Writings of Eugene V Debs

A Collection of Essays
by America's Most Famous Socialist

by Eugene V Debs

Red and Black Publishers, St Petersburg, Florida

Library of Congress Cataloging-in-Publication Data

Debs, Eugene V. (Eugene Victor), 1855-1926.
  Writings of Eugene V Debs : a collection of essays / by Eugene V Debs.
      p. cm.
  ISBN 978-1-934941-48-5
1. Debs, Eugene V. (Eugene Victor), 1855-1926--Correspondence. 2. Socialists--United
States--Correspondence. 3. Socialism--United States--History--Sources. 4. United States--
Politics and government--1865-1933--Sources. I. Title.
  HX84.D3D43 2009
  335'.3092--dc22
  [B]
                                                                    2008053364

Red and Black Publishers, PO Box 7542, St Petersburg, Florida, 33734

Contact us at: info@RedandBlackPublishers.com

Printed and manufactured in the United States of America

While there is a lower class I am in it;
While there is a criminal class I am of it;
While there is a soul in prison I am not free.

—Eugene V Debs

Contents

Life of Eugene V. Debs, Grand Secretary and Treasurer.

Published in Opening Exercises of the Fourteenth Annual Convention of the Brotherhood of Locomotive Firemen: Atlanta, Ga. Monday, September 10, 1888

At every convention of the Brotherhood of Locomotive Firemen, the remark is made by distinguished citizens invited to address the representatives of the Order, that the great majority are young men in the prime and strength of their young manhood. This is true — and when it is remembered that the Brotherhood, guided and controlled by young men since its birth in 1873, has been equal to every emergency and has achieved success, the fact bears testimony of capabilities of a high order and is fruitful of instructive reflections.

Eugene V. Debs, the subject of this sketch, the Grand Secretary and Treasurer of the Brotherhood of Locomotive

Firemen, was born in the city of Terre Haute, Indiana, November 5, 1855, and is now in the 33rd year of his age. His parents were natives of Alsace, once a province of France, where the love of liberty and independence characterized the people, as it has for a century. The great body of the French population in coming to the United States were not required to be educated to bring them into sympathy with American institutions and ideas, and as a consequence the boyhood home of Eugene was a place in which every lesson taught was well calculated to develop an ardent love of American ideas and principles of government.

At the proper age the boy was sent to the public schools of his native city and advanced through the various grades of the high school, from which he retired at the expiration of one year to enter a commercial college to obtain a thorough business education. Always distinguished for studious habits and the rapid acquisition of knowledge, he mastered his studies with a characteristic of genius and won the approval of his teachers.

At the age of 15 years, young Debs entered the Vandalia Railroad paint-shop as an apprentice. To the decorative art, while not distasteful, he preferred a more active life, and in 1871 accepted a position as fireman on a Vandalia locomotive, and continued to fire the machine till 1874. At 19 years of age he was tendered a position as clerk in the large wholesale house of Hulman & Co., of Terre Haute, in which he remained till 1879. At this time, the public career of Mr. Debs, then 24 years of age, began, and his great popularity in his native city was demonstrated by his triumphant election to the office of City Clerk by a majority of 1,100 over ten competitors. His first term in office was so distinguished by industry, ability, and integrity that he was reelected by an increased majority.

Though no longer handling pick and scoop in the cab, Mr. Debs did not permit his interest in the welfare of firemen to wane. He was initiated a member of Vigo Lodge, No. 16, February 27, 1874, and became one of its most active and efficient members. With a thorough business education obtained in college, in a large business house and in office, he brought to the Brotherhood a mind trained for practical work, an unbending will coupled with indefatigable power for work. He could with rare facility bring order out of confusion, and inspire confidence where doubt had gained ascendancy. This being true, it is not surprising that in the year 1877 he represented his lodge in the annual convention of the Order at Indianapolis, at a time when the Brotherhood was entering upon trials and vicissitudes that challenged all its resources of intelligence to maintain its position. In 1878 Mr. Debs was a delegate to the annual convention at Buffalo, where his services were of great value, as Assistant Secretary, and the Brotherhood, then recognizing his literary abilities, made him the associate editor of *The Locomotive Firemen's Magazine*.

In June 1880, Mr. Debs was appointed by the then Grand Master, F.W. Arnold, to the office of Grand Secretary and Treasurer of the Brotherhood, and in September 1880, he was elected to that office by the convention held in the city of Chicago, and has held the office since that date. In saying that Mr. Debs has displayed capacities of the highest order in conducting the office of Grand Secretary and Treasurer is simply echoing the verdict of the Brotherhood without a dissenting voice.

Since Mr. Debs assumed control of the office of Grand Secretary and Treasurer the Brotherhood has grown from 98 lodges to 384, with a corresponding increase of duties and responsibilities — and yet order, method, accuracy, and integrity have been maintained. Under his management of the finances of the brotherhood it has marched from despondency bordering upon despair, until in the pride of its strength the only question is, what shall be the sweep of its future victories.

This sketch of E.V. Debs, Grand Secretary and Treasurer, would be incomplete without special allusion to his connection with the *Locomotive Firemen's Magazine*, the organ of the Brotherhood. At the convention held in Boston, Mass. in 1881, Mr. Debs was elected editor of this publication. At that time its monthly circulation was about 3,000 copies, while at the present time it has reached the grand circulation of 30,000 copies. To say that such success is phenomenal is a tame expression, but the fact is eloquent of the tireless devotion of its editor to the duties of the arduous position and of his comprehensive knowledge of the education and literary wants of the Order.

In the year 1884 Mr. Debs was put in nomination by his fellow citizens of Vigo County for the responsible position of a representative in the Indiana Legislature to meet in January 1885. His great popularity and his mental endowments, together with his earnest defense of labor against the oppressions to which it had been subjected, marked him as the proper man to represent one of the most populous counties and one of the largest cities of the commonwealth, and he was triumphantly elected. His duties as a Legislator did not interfere with his duties to the Brotherhood, either as Grand Secretary or Treasurer or as the editor of the magazine.

In this connection it is worthy of remark that Mr. Debs was earnestly and time and again solicited to become a candidate for Congress, with every assurance of success, but his fealty to the great Brotherhood triumphed over the solicitations of political friends and every ambition for political distinction, and held him fast to the fortunes of the Brotherhood, in which by unwavering devotion and ceaseless labors for 8 years he had earned the confidence of the membership and flattering prominence.

Mr. Debs is now in the prime of his young manhood, and with hosts of friends and a happy home, the future holds out to him many dazzling prizes, to secure which he has only to put forth his mental and physical energies. As a writer, Mr. Debs has warmth, courage, and great versatility; his mind surveys the whole field of labor, and while devoted to the Brotherhood of which he is a member, he has generous words for other Brotherhoods and for all the toiling masses.

As a speaker, Mr. Debs is fluent, cogent, and persuasive, and often rising to height of eloquence, is greeted with appreciative applause. Affable and companionable, Mr. Debs wins friends and holds them in bonds which grow stronger the better he is known.

The Martyred Apostles of Labor

The New Time, February, 1898

The century now closing is luminous with great achievements. In every department of human endeavor marvelous progress has been made. By the magic of the machine which sprang from the inventive genius of man, wealth has been created in fabulous abundance. But, alas, this wealth, instead of blessing the race, has been the means of enslaving it. The few have come in possession of all, and the many have been reduced to the extremity of living by permission.

A few have had the courage to protest. To silence these so that the dead-level of slavery could be maintained has been the demand and command of capital-brown power. Press and pulpit responded with alacrity. All the forces of society were directed against these pioneers of industrial liberty, these brave defenders of oppressed humanity — and against them the crime of the century has been committed.

Albert R. Parsons, August Spies, George Engel, Adolph Fischer, Louis Lingg, Samuel Fielden, Michael Schwab and Oscar Neebe paid the cruel penalty in prison cell and on the gallows.

They were the first martyrs in the cause of industrial freedom, and one of the supreme duties of our civilization, if indeed we may boast of having been redeemed from savagery, is to rescue their names from calumny and do justice to their memory.

The crime with which these men were charged was never proven against them. The trial which resulted in their conviction was not only a disgrace to all judicial procedure but a foul, black, indelible and damning stigma upon the nation.

It was a trial organized and conducted to convict—a conspiracy to murder innocent men, and hence had not one redeeming feature.

It was a plot, satanic in all its conception, to wreak vengeance upon defenseless men, who, not being found guilty of the crime charged in the indictment, were found guilty of exercising the inalienable right of free speech in the interest of the toiling and groaning masses, and thus they became the first martyrs to a cause which, fertilized by their blood, has grown in strength and sweep and influence from the day they yielded up their lives and liberty in its defense.

As the years go by and the history of that infamous trial is read and considered by men of thought, who are capable of wrenching themselves from the grasp of prejudice and giving reason its rightful supremacy, the stronger the conviction becomes that the present generation of workingmen should erect an enduring memorial to the men who had the courage to denounce and oppose wage-slavery and seek for methods of emancipation.

The vision of the judicially murdered men was prescient. They saw the dark and hideous shadow of coming events. They spoke words of warning, not too soon, not too emphatic, not too trumpettoned—for even in 1886, when the Haymarket meetings were held, the capitalist grasp was upon the throats of workingmen and its fetters were upon their limbs.

There was even then idleness, poverty, squalor, the rattling of skeleton bones, the sunken eye, the pallor, the living death of famine, the crushing and the grinding of the relentless mills of the plutocracy, which more rapidly than the mills of the gods grind their victims to dust.

The men who went to their death upon the verdict of a jury, I have said, were judicially murdered—not only because the jury was packed for the express purpose of finding them guilty, not only because the crime for which they suffered was never proven against them, not only because the judge before whom they were arraigned was unjust and bloodthirsty, but because they had declared in the exercise of free speech that men who subjected their fellowmen to conditions often worse than death were unfit to live.

In all lands and in all ages where the victims of injustice have bowed their bodies to the earth, bearing grievous burdens laid upon them by cruel taskmasters, and have lifted their eyes starward in the hope of finding some orb whose light inspired hope, ten million times the anathema has been uttered and will be uttered until a day shall dawn upon the world when the emancipation of those who toil is achieved by the brave, self-sacrificing few who, like the Chicago martyrs, have the courage of crusaders and the spirit of iconoclasts and dare champion the cause of the oppressed and demand in the name of an avenging God and of an outraged Humanity that infernalism shall be eliminated from our civilization.

And as the struggle for justice proceeds and the battlefields are covered with the slain, as Mother Earth drinks their blood, the stones are given tongues with which to denounce man's inhumanity to man—aye, to women and cellar, arraign our civilization, our religion and our judiciary—whose wailings and lamentations, hushing to silence every sound the Creator designed to make the world a paradise of harmonies, transform it into an inferno where the demons of greed plot and scheme to consign their victims to lower depths of degradation and despair.

The men who were judicially murdered in Chicago in 1887, in the name of the great State of Illinois, were the *avant couriers* of a better day. They were called anarchists, but at their trial it was not proven that they had committed any crime or violated any law. They had protested against unjust laws and their brutal administration. They stood between oppressor and oppressed, and they dared, in a free (?) country, to exercise the divine right of free speech; and the records of their trial, as if written with an "iron pen and lead in the rock forever," proclaim the truth of the declaration.

I would rescue their names from slander. The slanderers of the dead are the oppressors of the living. I would, if I could, restore them to their rightful positions as evangelists, the proclaimers of good news to their fellowmen—crusaders, to rescue the sacred shrines of justice from the profanations of the capitalistic defilers who have made them more repulsive than Augean stables. Aye, I would take them, if I could, from peaceful slumber in their martyr graves—I would place joint to joint in their dislocated necks—I would make the halter the symbol of redemption—I would restore the flesh to their skeleton bones—their eyes should again flash defiance to the enemies of humanity, and their tongues, again, more eloquent than all the heroes of oratory, should speak the truth to a gainsaying world. Alas, this cannot be done—but something can be done. The stigma fixed upon their names by an outrageous trial can be forever obliterated and their fame be made to shine with resplendent glory on the pages of history.

Until the time shall come, as come it will, when the parks of Chicago shall be adorned with their statues, and with holy acclaim, men, women and children, pointing to these monuments as testimonial of gratitude, shall honor the men who dared to be true to humanity and paid the penalty of their heroism with their lives, the preliminary work of setting forth their virtues devolves upon those who are capable of gratitude to men who suffered death that they might live.

They were the men who, like Al-Hassen, the minstrel of the king, went forth to find themes of mirth and joy with which to gladden the ears of his master, but returned disappointed, and, instead of themes to awaken the gladness and joyous echoes, found scenes which dried all the fountains of joy. Touching his golden harp, Al-Hassen sang to the king as Parsons, Spies, Engels, Fielden, Fischer, Lingg, Schwab and Neebe proclaimed to the people:

"O king, at thy Command I went into the world of men; I sought full earnestly the thing which I Might weave into the gay and lightsome song. I found it, king; 'twas there. Had I the art To look but on the fair outside, I nothing Else had found. That art not mine, I saw what Lay beneath. And seeing thus I could not sing; For there, in dens more vile than wolf or jackal Ever sought, were herded, stifling, foul, the Writhing, crawling masses of mankind. Man! Ground down beneath oppression's iron heel, Till God in him was crushed and driven back, And only that which with the brute he shares Finds room to upward grow."

Such pictures of horror our martyrs saw in Chicago, as others have seen them in all the great centers of population in the country. But, like the noble minstrel, they proceeded to recite their discoveries and with him moaned:

"And in this world I saw how womanhood's fair flower had Never space its petals to unfold. How Childhood's tender bud was crushed and trampled Down in mire and filth too evil, foul, for beasts To be partaken in. For gold I saw The virgin sold, and motherhood was made A mock and score.

"I saw the fruit of labor Torn away from him who toiled, to further Swell the bursting coffers of the rich, while Babes and mothers pined and died of want. I saw dishonor and injustice thrive. I saw The wicked, ignorant, greedy, and unclean, By means of bribes and baseness, raised to seats Of power, from whence with lashes pitiless And keen, they scourged the hungry, naked throng Whom first they robbed and then enslaved."

Such were the scenes that the Chicago martyrs had witnessed and which may still be seen, and for reciting them and protesting against them they were judicially murdered.

It was not strange that the hearts of the martyrs "grew into one with the great moaning, throbbing heart" of the oppressed; not strange that the nerves of the martyrs grew "tense and quivering with the throes of mortal pain"; not strange that they should pity and plead and protest. The strange part of it is that in our high-noon of civilization a damnable judicial conspiracy should have been concocted to murder them under the forms of law.

That such is the truth of history, no honest man will attempt to deny; hence the demand, growing more pronounced every day, to snatch the names of these martyred evangelists of labor emancipation from dishonor and add them to the roll of the most illustrious dead of the nation.

Outlook for Socialism in the United States

International Socialist Review, September, 1900

The sun of the passing century is setting upon scenes of extraordinary activity in almost every part of our capitalistic old planet. Wars and rumors of wars are of universal prevalence. In the Philippines our soldiers are civilizing and Christianizing the natives in the latest and most approved styles of the art, and at prices ($13 per month) which command the blessing to the prayerful consideration of the lowly and oppressed everywhere.

In South Africa the British legions are overwhelming the Boers with volleys of benedictions inspired by the same beautiful philanthropy in the name of the meek and lowly Nazarene; while in China the heathen hordes, fanned into frenzy by the sordid spirit of modern commercial conquest, are presenting to the world a carnival of crime almost equaling the "refined" exhibitions of the world's "civilized" nations.

And through all the flame and furor of the fray can be heard the savage snarlings of the Christian "dogs of war" as they fiercely glare about them, and with jealous fury threaten to fly at one another's throats to settle the question of supremacy and the spoil and plunder of conquest.

The picture, lurid as a chamber of horrors, becomes complete in its gruesome ghastliness when robed ministers of Christ solemnly declare that it is all for the glory of God and the advancement of Christian civilization.

This, then, is the closing scene of the century as the curtain slowly descends upon the blood-stained stage—the central figure, the pious Wilhelm, Germany's sceptered savage, issuing his imperial "spare none" decree in the sang froid of an Apache chief—a fitting climax to the rapacious regime of the capitalist system.

Cheerless indeed would be the contemplation of such sanguinary scenes were the light of Socialism not breaking upon mankind. The skies of the East are even now aglow with the dawn; its coming is heralded by the dispelling of shadows, of darkness and gloom. From the first tremulous scintillation that guilds the horizon to the sublime march to meridian splendor the light increases till in mighty flood it pours upon the world.

From out of the midnight of superstition, ignorance and slavery the disenthralling, emancipating sun is rising. I am not gifted with prophetic vision, and yet I see the shadows vanishing. I behold near and far prostrate men lifting their bowed forms from the dust. I see thrones in the grasp of decay; despots relaxing their hold upon scepters, and shackles falling, not only from the limbs, but from the souls of men.

It is therefore with pleasure that I respond to the invitation of the editor of the *International Socialist Review* to present my views upon the "Outlook for Socialism in the United States." Socialists generally will agree that the past year has been marked with a propaganda of unprecedented activity and that the sentiment of the American people in respect to Socialism has undergone a most remarkable change. It should be difficult to imagine a more ignorant, bitter and unreasoning prejudice than that of the American people against Socialism during the early years of its introduction by the propagandists from the other side.

I never think of these despised and persecuted "foreign invaders" without a feeling of profound obligation, akin to reverence, for their noble work in laying the foundations deep and strong, under the most trying conditions, of the American movement. The ignorant mass, wholly incapable of grasping their splendid teachings or appreciating their lofty motives, reviled against them. The press inoculated the public sentiment with intolerance and malice which not infrequently found expression through the policeman's club when a few of the pioneers gathered to engraft the class-conscious doctrine upon their inhospitable "free-born" American fellow citizens.

Socialism was cunningly associated with "anarchy and bloodshed" and denounced as a "foul foreign importation" to pollute the fair, free soil of America, and every outrage to which the early agitators were subjected won the plaudits of the people. But they persevered in their task; they could not be silenced or suppressed. Slowly they increased in number and gradually the movement began to take root and spread over the country. The industrial conditions consequent upon the development of capitalist production were now making themselves felt and Socialism became a fixed and increasing factor in the economic and political affairs of the nation.

The same difficulties which other countries had experienced in the process of party organization have attended the development of the movement here, but these differences, which relate mainly to tactics and methods of propaganda, are bound to disappear as the friction of the jarring factions smoothens out the rough edges and adjusts them to a concrete body—a powerful section in the great international army of militant Socialism.

In the general elections of 1898 upwards of 91,000 votes were cast for the Socialist candidate of the United States, an increase in this "off year" of almost two hundred per cent over the general elections of two years previous, the presidential year of 1896. Since the congressional elections of 1898, and more particularly since the municipal and state elections following, which resulted in such signal victories in Massachusetts, two members of the legislature and a mayor, the first in America, being elected by decided majorities—since then Socialism has made rapid strides in all directions and the old politicians no longer reckon it as a negative quantity in making their forecasts and calculating their pluralities and majorities.

The subject has passed entirely beyond the domain of sneer and ridicule and now commands serious treatment. Of course, Socialism is violently denounced by the capitalist press and by all the brood of subsidized contributors to magazine literature, but this only confirms the view that the advance of Socialism is very properly recognized by the capitalist class as the one cloud upon the horizon which portends an end to the system in which they have waxed fat, insolent and despotic through the exploitation of their countless wage-working slaves.

In school and college and church, in clubs and public halls everywhere, Socialism is the central theme of discussion, and its advocates, inspired by its noble principles, are to be found here, there and in all places ready to give or accept challenge to battle. In the cities the corner meetings are popular and effective. But rarely is such a gathering now molested by the "authorities," and then only where they have just been inaugurated. They are too numerously attended by serious, intelligent and self-reliant men and women to invite interference.

Agitation is followed by organization, and the increase of branches, sections and clubs goes forward with extraordinary activity in every part of the land.

In New England the agitation has resulted in quite a general organization among the states, with Massachusetts in the lead; and the indications are that, with the vigorous prosecution of the campaign already inaugurated, a tremendous increase in the vote will be polled in the approaching national elections. New York and Pennsylvania will show surprising Socialist returns, while Ohio, Michigan, Indiana, Illinois, Missouri and Kentucky will all round up with a large vote. Wisconsin has already a great vote to her credit and will increase it largely this year. In the west and northwest, Kansas, Iowa and Minnesota will forge to the front, and so also will Nebraska, the Dakotas, Montana, Oregon, Washington, Idaho and Colorado. California is expected to show an immense increase, and the returns from there will not disappoint the most sanguine. In the southwest, Texas is making a stirring campaign, and several papers, heretofore Populist, will support our candidates and swell the socialist vote, which will be an eye-opener when announced.

On the whole, the situation could scarcely be more favorable and the final returns will more than justify our sanguine expectations.

It must not be overlooked, however, when calculations are made, that this is a presidential year and that the general results will not be so favorable as if the elections were in an "off year." Both the Republican and Democratic parties will, as usual, strain every nerve to whip the "voting kings" into line and every conceivable influence will be exerted to that end. These vast machines operate with marvelous precision and the wheels are already in motion. Corruption funds, national, state and municipal, will flow out like lava tides; promises will be as plentiful as autumn leaves; from ten thousand platforms the Columbian orator will agitate the atmosphere, while brass bands, torchlight processions, glittering uniforms and free whisky, dispensed by the "ward-heeler," will lend their combined influence to steer the "patriots" to the capitalist chute that empties into the ballot box.

The campaign this year will be unusually spectacular. The Republican party "points with pride" to the "prosperity" and the "war record" of the administration. The Democratic party declares that "imperialism" is the "paramount" issue, and that the country is certain to go to the "damnation bow-wows" if Democratic officeholders are not elected instead of the Republicans. The Democratic slogan is "The Republican vs. the Empire," accompanied in a very minor key by 16 to 1 and "direct legislation where practical."

Both these capitalist parties are fiercely opposed to trusts, though what they propose to do with them is not of sufficient importance to require even a hint in their platforms.

Needless is it for me to say to the thinking workingman that he has no choice between these two capitalist parties, that they are both pledged to the same system and that whether the one or the other succeeds, he will still remain the wage-working slave he is today.

What but meaningless phrases are "imperialism," "expansion," "free silver," "gold standard," etc., to the wage-worker? The large capitalists represented by Mr. McKinley and the small capitalists represented by Mr. Bryan are interested in these "issues," but they do not concern the working class.

What the workingmen of the country are profoundly interested in is the private ownership of the means of production and distribution, the enslaving and degrading wage-system in which they toil for a pittance at the pleasure of their masters and are bludgeoned, jailed or shot when they protest—this is the central, controlling, vital issue of the hour, and neither of the old party platforms has a word or even a hint about it.

As a rule, large capitalists are Republicans and small capitalists are Democrats, but workingmen must remember that they are all capitalists, and that the many small ones, like the fewer large ones, are all politically supporting their class interests, and this is always and everywhere the capitalist class.

Whether the means of production—that is to say, the land, mines, factories, machinery, etc.—are owned by a few large Republican capitalists, who organize a trust, or whether they be owned by a lot of small Democratic capitalists, who are opposed to the trust, is all the same to the working class. Let the capitalists, large and small, fight this out among themselves.

The working class must get rid of the whole brood of masters and exploiters, and put themselves in possession and control of the means of production, that they may have steady employment without consulting a capitalist employer, large or small, and that they may get the wealth their labor produces, all of it, and enjoy with their families the fruits of their industry in comfortable and happy homes, abundant and wholesome food, proper clothing and all other things necessary to "life, liberty and the pursuit of happiness." It is therefore a question not of "reform," the mask of fraud, but of revolution. The capitalist system must be overthrown, class-rule abolished and wage-slavery supplanted by the cooperative industry.

We hear it frequently urged that the Democratic party is the "poor man's party," "the friend of labor." There is but one way to relieve poverty and to free labor, and that is by making common property of the tools of labor.

Is the Democratic party, which we are assured has "strong socialistic tendencies," in favor of collective ownership of the means of production? Is it opposed to the wage-system, from which flows in a ceaseless stream the poverty, misery and wretchedness of the children of toil? If the Democratic party is the "friend of labor" any more than the Republican party, why is its platform dumb in the presence of Cœur d'Alene? It knows the truth about these shocking outrages—crimes upon workingmen, their wives and children, which would blacken the pages of Siberia—why does it not speak out?

What has the Democratic party to say about the "property and educational qualifications" in North Carolina and Louisiana, and the proposed general disfranchisement of the negro race in the southern states?

The difference between the Republican and Democratic parties involve no issue, no principle in which the working class have any interest, and whether the spoils be distributed by Hanna and Platt, or by Croker and Tammany Hall is all the same to them.

Between these parties Socialists have no choice, no preference. They are one in their opposition to Socialism, that is to say, the emancipation of the working class from wage-slavery, and every workingman who has intelligence enough to understand the interest of his class and the nature of the struggle in which it is involved, will once and for all time sever his relations with them both; and recognizing the class-struggle which is being waged between the producing workers and non-producing capitalists, cast his lot with the class-conscious, revolutionary Socialist party, which is pledged to abolish the capitalist system, class-rule and wage-slavery—a party which does not compromise or fuse, but, preserving inviolate the principles which quickened it into life and now give it vitality and force, moves forward with dauntless determination to the goal of economic freedom.

The political trend is steadily toward Socialism. The old parties are held together only by the cohesive power of spoils, and in spite of this they are steadily disintegrating. Again and again they have been tried with the same results, and thousands upon thousands awake to their duplicity, are deserting them and turning toward the Socialism as the only refuge and security. Republicans, Democrats, Populists, Prohibitionists, Single Taxers are having their eyes opened to the true nature of the struggle and they are beginning to

"Come as the winds come, when Forests are rended;
Come as the waves come, when Navies are stranded."

For a time the Populist party had a mission, but it is practically ended. The Democratic party has "fused" it out of existence. The "middle-of-the-road" element will be sorely disappointed when the votes are counted, and they will probably never figure in another national campaign. Not many of them will go back to the old parties. Many of them have already come to Socialism, and they rest are sure to follow.

There is no longer any room for a Populist party, and progressive Populists realize it, and hence the "strongholds" of Populism are becoming "hot-beds" of Socialism.

It is simply a question of capitalism or socialism, of despotism or democracy, and they who are not wholly with us are wholly against us.

Another source of strength to Socialism, steadily increasing, is the trade-union movement. The spread of Socialist doctrine among the labor organizations of the country during the past year exceeds the most extravagant estimates. No one has had better opportunities than the writer to note the transition to Socialism among trades-unionists, and the approaching election will abundantly verify it.

Promising, indeed, is the outlook for Socialism in the United States. The very contemplation of the prospect is a well-spring of inspiration.

Oh, that all the working class could and would use their eyes and see; their ears and hear; their brains and think. How soon this earth could be transformed and by the alchemy of social order made to blossom with beauty and joy.

No sane man can be satisfied with the present system. If a poor man is happy, said Victor Hugo, "he is the pick-pocket of happiness. Only the rich and noble are happy by right. The rich man is he who, being young, has the rights of old age; being old, the lucky chances of youth; vicious, the respect of good people; a coward, the command of the stout-hearted; doing nothing, the fruits of labor."

With pride and joy we watch each advancing step of our comrades in Socialism in all other lands. Our hearts are with them in their varying fortunes as the battle proceeds, and we applaud each telling blow delivered and cheer each victory achieved.

The wire has just brought the tidings of Liebknecht's death. The hearts of American Socialists will be touched and shocked by the calamity. The brave old warrior succumbed at last, but not until he heard the tramp of International Socialism, for which he labored with all his loving, loyal heart; not until he saw the thrones of Europe, one by one, begin to totter, not until he had achieved a glorious immortality.

How I Became a Socialist

New York Comrade, April, 1902

As I have some doubt about the readers of *The Comrade* having any curiosity as to "how I became a Socialist" it may be in order to say that the subject is the editor's, not my own; and that what is here offered is at his bidding—my only concern being that he shall not have cause to wish that I had remained what I was instead of becoming a Socialist.

On the evening of February 27, 1875, the local lodge of the Brotherhood of Locomotive Firemen was organized at Terre

Haute, Ind., by Joshua A. Leach, then grand master, and I was admitted as a charter member and at once chosen secretary. "Old Josh Leach," as he was affectionately called, a typical locomotive fireman of his day, was the founder of the brotherhood, and I was instantly attracted by his rugged honesty, simple manner and homely speech. How well I remember felling his large, rough hand on my shoulder, the kindly eye of an elder brother searching my own as he gently said, "My boy, you're a little young, but I believe you're in earnest and will make your mark in the brotherhood." Of course, I assured him that I would do my best. What he really thought at the time flattered my boyish vanity not a little when I heard of it. He was attending a meeting at St. Louis some months later, and in the course of his remarks said: "I put a tow-headed boy in the brotherhood at Terre Haute not long ago, and some day he will be at the head of it."

Twenty-seven years, to a day, have played their pranks with "Old Josh" and the rest of us. When last we met, not long ago, and I pressed his good, right hand, I observed that he was crowned with the front that never melts; and as I think of him now:

"Remembrance wakes, with all her busy train,
Swells at my breast and turns the past to pain."

My first step was thus taken in organized labor and a new influence fired my ambition and changed the whole current of my career. I was filled with enthusiasm and my blood fairly leaped in my veins. Day and night I worked for the brotherhood. To see its watchfires glow and observe the increase of its sturdy members were the sunshine and shower of my life. To attend the "meeting" was my supreme joy, and for ten years I was not once absent when the faithful assembled.

At the convention held in Buffalo in 1878 I was chosen associate editor of the magazine, and in 1880 I became grand secretary and treasurer. With all the fire of youth I entered upon the crusade which seemed to fairly glitter with possibilities. For eighteen hours at a stretch I was glued to my desk reeling off the answers to my many correspondents. Day and night were one. Sleep was time wasted and often, when all oblivious of her presence in the still small hours my mother's hand turned off the light, I went to bed under protest. Oh, what days! And what quenchless zeal and consuming vanity! All the firemen everywhere — and they were all the world — were straining:

"To catch the beat
On my tramping feet."

My grip was always packed; and I was darting in all directions. To tramp through a railroad yard in the rain, snow or sleet half the night, or till daybreak, to be ordered out of the roundhouse for being an "agitator," or put off a train, sometimes passenger, more often freight, while attempting to deadhead over the division, were all in the program, and served to whet the appetite to conquer. One night in midwinter at Elmira, N. Y., a conductor on the Erie kindly dropped me off in a snowbank, and as I clambered to the top I ran into the arms of a policeman, who heard my story and on the spot became my friend.

I rode on the engines over mountain and plain, slept in the cabooses and bunks, and was fed from their pails by the swarthy stokers who still nestle close to my heart, and will until it is cold and still.

Through all these years I was nourished at Fountain Proletaire. I drank deeply of its waters and every particle of my tissue became saturated with the spirit of the working class. I had fired an engine and been stung by the exposure and hardship of the rail. I was with the boys in their weary watches, at the broken engine's side and often helped to bear their bruised and bleeding bodies back to wife and child again. How could I but feel the burden of their wrongs? How the seed of agitation fail to take deep root in my heart?

And so I was spurred on in the work of organizing, not the fireman merely, but the brakemen, switchmen, telegraphers, shopmen, track-hands, all of them in fact, and as I had now become known as an organizer, the calls came from all sides and there are but few trades I have not helped to organize and less still in whose strikes I have not at some time had a hand.

In 1894 the American Railway Union was organized and a braver body of men never fought the battle of the working class.

Up to this time I had heard but little of Socialism, knew practically nothing about the movement, and what little I did know was not calculated to impress me in its favor. I was bent on thorough and complete organization of the railroad men and ultimately the whole working class, and all my time and energy were given to that end. My supreme conviction was that if they were only organized in every branch of the service and all acted together in concert they could redress their wrongs and regulate the conditions of their employment. The stockholders of the corporation acted as one, why not the men? It was such a plain proposition—simply to follow the example set before their eyes by their masters—surely they could not fail to see it, act as one, and solve the problem.

It is useless to say that I had yet to learn the workings of the capitalist system, the resources of its masters and the weakness of its slaves. Indeed, no shadow of a "system" fell athwart my pathway; no thought of ending wage-misery marred my plans. I was too deeply absorbed in perfecting wage-servitude and making it a "thing of beauty and a joy forever."

It all seems very strange to me now, taking a backward look, that my vision was so focalized on a single objective point that I utterly failed to see what now appears as clear as the noonday sun—so clear that I marvel that any workingman, however dull, uncomprehending, can resist it.

But perhaps it was better so. I was to be baptized in Socialism in the roar of conflict and I thank the gods for reserving to this fitful occasion the fiat, "Let there be light!" — the light that streams in steady radiance upon the broadway to the Socialist republic.

The skirmish lines of the A. R. U. were well advanced. A series of small battles were fought and won without the loss of a man. A number of concessions were made by the corporations rather than risk an encounter. Then came the fight on the Great Northern, short sharp, and decisive. The victory was complete—the only railroad strike of magnitude ever won by an organization in America.

Next followed the final shock—the Pullman strike—and the American Railway Union again won, clear and complete. The combined corporations were paralyzed and helpless. At this juncture there were delivered, from wholly unexpected quarters, a swift succession of blows that blinded me for an instant and then opened wide my eyes—and in the gleam of every bayonet and the flash of every rifle the class struggle was revealed. This was my first practical lesson in Socialism, though wholly unaware that it was called by that name.

An army of detectives, thugs and murderers were equipped with badge and beer and bludgeon and turned loose; old hulks of cars were fired; the alarm bells tolled; the people were terrified; the most startling rumors were set afloat; the press volleyed and thundered, and over all the wires sped the news that Chicago's white throat was in the clutch of a red mod; injunctions flew thick and fast, arrests followed, and our office and headquarters, the heart of the strike, was sacked, torn out and nailed up by the "lawful" authorities of the federal government; and when in company with my loyal comrades I found myself in Cook county jail at Chicago with the whole press screaming conspiracy, treason and murder, and by some fateful coincidence I was given the cell occupied just previous to his execution by the assassin of Mayor Carter Harrison, Sr., overlooking the spot, a few feet distant, where anarchists were hanged a few years before, I had another exceedingly practical and impressive lesson in Socialism.

Acting upon the advice of friends we sought to employ John Harlan, son of the Supreme Justice, to assist in our defense—a defense memorable to me chiefly because of the skill and fidelity of our lawyers, among whom were the brilliant Clarence Darrow and the venerable Judge Lyman Trumbull, author of the thirteenth amendment to the Constitution, abolishing slavery in the United States.

Mr. Harlan wanted to think of the matter over night; and the next morning gravely informed us that he could not afford to be identified with the case, "for," said he, "you will be tried upon the same theory as were the anarchists, with probably the same result." That day, I remember, the jailer, by way of consolation, I suppose, showed us the blood-stained rope used at the last execution and explained in minutest detail, as he exhibited the gruesome relic, just how the monstrous crime of lawful murder is committed.

But the tempest gradually subsided and with it the bloodthirstiness of the press and "public sentiment." We were not sentenced to the gallows, nor ever to the penitentiary — though put on trial for conspiracy — for reasons that will make another story.

The Chicago jail sentences were followed by six months at Woodstock and it was here that Socialism gradually laid hold of me in its own irresistible fashion. Books and pamphlets and letters from socialists came by every mail and I began to read and think and dissect the anatomy of the system in which workingmen, however organized, could be shattered and battered and splintered at a single stroke. The writings of Bellamy and Blanchford early appealed to me. The "Cooperative Commonwealth" of Gronlund also impressed me, but the writings of Kautsky were so clear and conclusive that I readily grasped, not merely his argument, but also caught the spirit of his socialist utterance — and I thank him and all who helped me out of darkness into light.

It was at this time, when the first glimmerings of Socialism were beginning to penetrate, that Victor L. Berger — and I have loved him ever since — came to Woodstock, as if a providential instrument, and delivered the first impassioned message of Socialism I had ever heard — the very first to set the "wires humming in my system." As a souvenir of that visit there is in my library a volume of *Capital*, by Karl Marx, inscribed with the compliments of Victor L. Berger, which I cherish as a token of priceless value.

The American Railway Union was defeated but not conquered—overwhelmed but not destroyed. It lives and pulsates in the Socialist movement, and its defeat but blazed the way to economic freedom and hastened the dawn of human brotherhood.

Danger Ahead

International Socialist Review, Vol. IV, No. 5. November 1903

It so happens that I write upon the Negro question, in compliance with the request of the editor of the *International Socialist Review*, in the state of Louisiana, where the race prejudice is as strong and the feeling against the "nigger" as bitter and relentless as when Lincoln's proclamation of emancipation lashed the waning Confederacy into fury and incited the final and desperate attempts to burst the bonds that held the southern states in the federal union. Indeed, so thoroughly is the south permeated with the malign spirit of race hatred that even Socialists are to be found, and by no means rarely, who either share directly in the race hostility against the Negro, or avoid the issue, or apologize for the social obliteration of the color line in the class struggle.

The white man in the south declares that "the nigger is all right in his place"; that is, as menial, servant and slave. If he dare hold up his head, feel the thrill of manhood in his veins and nurse the hope that some day may bring deliverance; if in his brain the thought of freedom dawns and in his heart the aspiration to rise above the animal plane and propensities of his sires, he must be made to realize that notwithstanding the white man is civilized (?) the black man is a "nigger" still and must so remain as long as planets wheel in space.

But while the white man is considerate enough to tolerate the Negro "in his place," the remotest suggestion at social recognition arouses all the pent-up wrath of his Anglo-Saxon civilization; and my observation is that the less real ground there is for such indignant assertion of self -superiority, the more passionately it is proclaimed.

At Yoakum, Texas, a few days ago, leaving the depot with two grips in my hands, I passed four or five bearers of the white man's burden perched on a railing and decorating their environment with tobacco juice. One of them, addressing me, said: "There's a nigger that'll carry your grips." A second one added: "That's what he's here for," and the third chimed in with "That's right, by God." Here was a savory bouquet of white superiority. One glance was sufficient to satisfy me that they represented all there is of justification for the implacable hatred of the Negro race. They were ignorant, lazy, unclean, totally void of ambition, themselves the foul product of the capitalist system and held in lowest contempt by the master class, yet esteeming themselves immeasurably above the cleanest, most intelligent and self-respecting Negro, having by reflex absorbed the "nigger" hatred of their masters.

As a matter of fact the industrial supremacy of the south before the war would not have been possible without the Negro, and the south of today would totally collapse without his labor. Cotton culture has been and is the great staple and it will not be denied that the fineness and superiority of the fibre that makes the export of the southern states the greatest in the world is due in large measure to the genius of the Negroes charged with its cultivation.

The whole world is under obligation to the Negro, and that the white heel is still upon the black neck is simply proof that the world is not yet civilized.

The history of the Negro in the United States is a history of crime without a parallel.

Why should the white man hate him? Because he stole him from his native land and for two centuries and a half robbed him of the fruit of his labor, kept him in beastly ignorance and subjected him to the brutal domination of the lash? Because he tore the black child from the breast of its mother and ravished the black man's daughter before her father's eyes?

There are thousands of Negroes who bear testimony in their whitening skins that men who so furiously resent the suggestion of "social equality" are far less sensitive in respect to the sexual equality of the races.

But of all the senseless agitation in capitalist society, that in respect to "social equality" takes the palm. The very instant it is mentioned the old aristocratic plantation owner's shrill cry about the "buck nigger" marrying the "fair young daughter" of his master is heard from the tomb and echoed and re-echoed across the spaces and repeated by the "white trash" in proud vindication of their social superiority.

Social equality, forsooth! Is the black man pressing his claims for social recognition upon his white burden bearer? Is there any reason why he should? Is the white man's social recognition of his own white brother such as to excite the Negro's ambition to covet the noble prize? Has the Negro any greater desire, or is there any reason why he should have, for social intercourse with the white man than the white man has for social relations with the Negro? This phase of the Negro question is pure fraud and serves to mask the real issue, which is not social equality, *but economic freedom*.

There never was any social inferiority that was not the shriveled fruit of economic inequality.

The Negro, given economic freedom, will not ask the white man any social favors; and the burning question of "social equality" will disappear like mist before the sunrise.

I have said and say again that, properly speaking, there is no Negro question outside of the labor question—the working class struggle. Our position as Socialists and as a party is perfectly plain. We have simply to say: "The class struggle is colorless." The capitalists, white, black and other shades, are on one side and the workers, white, black and all other colors, on the other side.

When Marx said: "Workingmen of all countries unite," he gave concrete expression to the socialist philosophy of the class struggle; unlike the framers of the Declaration of Independence who announced that "all men are created equal" and then basely repudiated their own doctrine, Marx issued the call to all the workers of the globe, regardless of race, sex, creed or any other condition whatsoever.

As a social party we receive the Negro and all other races upon absolutely equal terms. We are the party of the working class, the whole working class, and we will not suffer ourselves to be divided by any specious appeal to race prejudice; and if we should be coaxed or driven from the straight road we will be lost in the wilderness and ought to perish there, for we shall no longer be a Socialist party.

Let the capitalist press and capitalist "public opinion" indulge themselves in alternate flattery and abuse of the Negro; we as Socialists will receive him in our party, treat him in our counsels and stand by him all around the same as if his skin were white instead of black; and this we do, not from any considerations of sentiment, but because it accords with the philosophy of Socialism, the genius of the class struggle, and is eternally right and bound to triumph in the end.

With the "nigger" question, the "race war" from the capitalist viewpoint, we have nothing to do. In capitalism the Negro question is a grave one and will grow more threatening as the contradictions and complications of capitalist society multiply, but this need not worry us. Let them settle the Negro question in their way, if they can. We have nothing to do with it, for that is their fight. We have simply to open the eyes of as many Negroes as we can and bring them into the Socialist movement to do battle for emancipation from wage slavery, and when the working class have triumphed in the class struggle and stand forth economic as well as political free men, the race problem will forever disappear.

Socialists should with pride proclaim their sympathy with and fealty to the black race, and if any there be who hesitate to avow themselves in the face of ignorant and unreasoning prejudice, they lack the true spirit of the slavery-destroying revolutionary movement.

The voice of Socialism must be as inspiring music to the ears of those in bondage, especially the weak black brethren, doubly enslaved, who are bowed to the earth and groan in despair beneath the burden of the centuries.

For myself, my heart goes to the Negro and I make no apology to any white man for it. In fact, when I see the poor, brutalized, outraged black victim, I feel a burning sense of guilt for his intellectual poverty and moral debasement that makes me blush for the unspeakable crimes committed by my own race.

In closing, permit me to express the hope that the next convention may repeal the resolutions on the Negro question. The Negro does not need them and they serve to increase rather than diminish the necessity for explanation.

We have nothing special to offer the Negro, and we cannot make separate appeals to all the races.

The Socialist Party is the party of the working class, regardless of color—the whole working class of the whole world.

The Socialist Party and the Working Class

Opening Speech Delivered as Candidate of the Socialist Party for the President at Indianapolis, Ind., September 1, 1904

Mr. Chairman, Citizens and Comrades:

There has never been a free people, a civilized nation, a real republic on this earth. Human society has always consisted of masters and slaves, and the slaves have always been and are today, the foundation stones of the social fabric.

Wage-labor is but a name; wage-slavery is the fact.

The twenty-five millions of wage-slavery in the United States are twenty-five millions of twentieth century slaves.

This is the plain meaning of what is known as the Labor Market.

And the labor market follows the capitalist flag.

The most barbarous fact in all christendom is the labor market. The mere term sufficiently expresses the animalism of commercial civilization.

They who buy and they who sell in the labor market are alike dehumanized by the inhuman traffic in the brains and blood and bones of human beings.

The labor market is the foundation of so-called civilized society. Without these shambles, without this commerce in human life, this sacrifice of manhood and womanhood, this barter of babes, this sales of souls, the capitalist civilizations of all lands and all climes would crumble to ruin and perish from the earth.

Twenty-five millions of wage-slaves are bought and sold daily at prevailing prices in the American Labor Market. This is the paramount issue in the present national campaign.

Let me say at the very threshold of this discussion that the workers have but the one issue in this campaign, the overthrow of the capitalist system and the emancipation of the working class from wage-slavery.

The capitalists may have the tariff, finance, imperialism and other dust-covered and moth-eaten issues entirely to themselves.

The rattle of these relics no longer deceives workingmen whose heads are on their own shoulders.

They know by experience and observation that the gold standard, free silver, fiat money, protective tariff, free trade, imperialism and anti-imperialism. all mean capitalist rule and wage-slavery.

Their eyes are open and they can see; their brains are in operation and they can think.

The very moment a workingman begins to do his own thinking he understands the paramount issue, parts company with the capitalist politician and falls in line with his own class on the political battlefield.

The political solidarity of the working class means the death of despotism, the birth of freedom, the sunrise of civilization.

Having said this much by way of introduction I will now enter upon the actualities of my theme.

THE CLASS STRUGGLE

We are entering tonight upon a momentous campaign. The struggle for political supremacy is not between political parties merely, as appears upon the surface, but at bottom it is a life and death struggle between two hostile economic classes, the one the capitalist, and the other the working class.

The capitalist class is represented by the Republican, Democratic, Populist and Prohibition parties, all of which stand for private ownership of the means of production, and the triumph of any one of which will mean continued wage-slavery to the working class.

As the Populist and Prohibition sections of the capitalist party represent minority elements which propose to reform the capitalist system without disturbing wage-slavery, a vain and impossible task, they will be omitted from this discussion with all the credit due the rank and file for their good intentions.

The Republican and Democratic parties, or, to be more exact, the Republican-Democratic party, represent the capitalist class in the class struggle. They are the political wings of the capitalist system and such differences as arise between them relate to spoils and not to principles.

With either of those parties in power one thing is always certain and that is that the capitalist class is in the saddle and the working class under the saddle.

Under the administration of both these parties the means of production are private property, production is carried forward for capitalist profit purely, markets are glutted and industry paralyzed, workingmen become tramps and criminals while injunctions, soldiers and riot guns are brought into action to preserve "law and order" in the chaotic carnival of capitalistic anarchy.

Deny it as may the cunning capitalists who are clear-sighted enough to perceive it, or ignore it as may the torpid workers who are too blind and unthinking to see it, the struggle in which we are engaged today is a class struggle, and as the toiling millions come to see and understand it and rally to the political standard of their class, they will drive all capitalist parties of whatever name into the same party, and the class struggle will then be so clearly revealed that the hosts of labor will find their true place in the conflict and strike the united and decisive blow that will destroy slavery and achieve their full and final emancipation.

In this struggle the workingmen and women and children are represented by the Socialist party and it is my privilege to address you in the name of that revolutionary and uncompromising party of the working class.

ATTITUDE OF THE WORKERS

What shall be the attitude of the workers of the United States in the present campaign? What part shall they take in it? What party and what principles shall they support by their ballots? And why?

These are questions the importance of which are not sufficiently recognized by workingmen, or they would not be the prey of parasites and the service tools of scheming politicians who use them only at election time to renew their masters" lease of power and perpetuate their own ignorance, poverty and shame.

In answering these questions I propose to be as frank and candid as plain-meaning words will allow, for I have but one object in this discussion and that object is not office, but the truth, and I shall state it as I see it, if I have to stand alone.

But I shall not stand alone, for the party that has my allegiance and may have my life, the Socialist party, the party of the working class, the party of emancipation, is made up of men and women who know their rights and scorn to compromise with their oppressors; who want no votes that can be bought and no support under any false pretense whatsoever.

The Socialist party stands squarely upon its proletarian principles and relies wholly upon the forces of industrial progress and the education of the working class.

The Socialist party buys no votes and promises no offices. Not a farthing is spent for whiskey or cigars. Every penny in the campaign fund is the voluntary offerings of workers and their sympathizers and every penny is used for education.

What other parties can say the same?

Ignorance alone stand in the way of socialist success. The capitalist parties understand this and use their resources to prevent the workers from seeing the light.

Intellectual darkness is essential to industrial slavery.

Capitalist parties stand for Slavery and Night.

The Socialist party is the herald of Freedom and Light.

Capitalist parties cunningly contrive to divide the workers upon dead issues.

The Socialist party is uniting them upon the living issue:

Death to Wage Slavery!

When industrial slavery is as dead as the issues of the Siamese capitalist parties the Socialist party will have fulfilled its mission and enriched history.

And now to our questions:

First, all workingmen and women owe it to themselves, their class and their country to take an active and intelligent interest in political affairs.

THE BALLOT

The ballot of united labor expresses the people's will and the people's will is the supreme law of a free nation.

The ballot means that labor is no longer dumb, that at last it has a voice, that it may be heard and if united shall be heeded.

Centuries of struggle and sacrifice were required to wrest this symbol of freedom from the mailed clutch of tyranny and place it in the hand of labor as the shield and lance of attack and defense.

The abuse and not the use of it is responsible for its evils.

The divided vote of labor is the abuse of the ballot and the penalty is slavery and death.

The united vote of those who toil and have not will vanquish those who have and toil not, and solve forever the problems of democracy.

THE HISTORIC STRUGGLE OF CLASSES

Since the human race was young there have been class struggles. In every state of society, ancient and modern, labor has been exploited, degraded and in subjection.

Civilization has done little for labor except to modify the forms of its exploitation.

Labor has always been the mudsill of the social fabric — is so now and will be until the class struggle ends in class extinction and free society.

Society has always been and is now built upon exploitation — the exploitation of a class — the working class, whether slaves, serfs or wage-laborers, and the exploited working class in subjection have always been, instinctively or consciously, in revolt against their oppressors.

Through all the centuries the enslaved toilers have moved slowly but surely toward their final freedom.

The call of the Socialist party is to the exploited class, the workers in all useful trades and professions, all honest occupations, from the most menial service to the highest skill, to rally beneath their own standard and put an end to the last of the barbarous class struggles by conquering the capitalist government, taking possession of the means of production and making them the common property of all, abolishing wage-slavery and establishing the co-operative commonwealth.

The first step in this direction is to sever all relations with the capitalist parties. They are precisely alike and I challenge their most discriminating partisans to tell them apart in relation to labor.

The Republican and Democratic parties are alike capitalist parties — differing only in being committed to different sets of capitalist interests — they have the same principles under varying colors, are equally corrupt and are one in their subservience to capital and their hostility to labor.

The ignorant workingman who supports either of these parties forges his own fetters and is the unconscious author of his own misery. He can and must be made to see and think and act with his fellows in supporting the party of his class and this work of education is the crowning virtue of the socialist movement.

THE REPUBLICAN PARTY

Let us briefly consider the Republican party from the worker's standpoint. It is capitalist to the core. It has not and can not have the slightest interest in labor except to exploit it.

Why should a workingman support the Republican party?

Why should a millionaire support the Socialist party?

For precisely the same reason that all the millionaires are opposed to the Socialist party, all workers should be opposed to the Republican party. It is a capitalist party, is loyal to capitalist interests and entitled to the support of capitalist voters on election day.

All it has for workingmen is its "glorious past" and a "glad hand" when it wants their votes.

The Republican party is now and has been for several years, in complete control of government.

What has it done for labor? What has it not done for capital?

Not one of the crying abuses of capital has been curbed under Republican rule.

Not one of the petitions of labor has been granted.

The eight hour and anti-injunction bills, upon which organized labor is a unit, were again ruthlessly slain by the last congress in obedience to the capitalist masters.

David M. Parry has greater influence at Washington than all the millions of organized workers.

Read the national platform of the Republican party and see if there is in all its bombast a crumb of comfort for labor. The convention that adopted it was a capitalist convention and the only thought it had of labor was how to abstract its vote without waking it up.

In the only reference it made to labor it had to speak easy so as to avoid offense to the capitalists who own it and furnish the boodle to keep it in power.

The labor platforms of the Republican and Democratic parties are interchangeable and non-redeemable. They both favor "justice to capital and justice to labor." This hoary old platitude is worse than meaningless. It is false and misleading and so intended. Justice to labor means that labor shall have what it produces. This leaves nothing for capital.

Justice to labor means the end of capital.

The old parties intend nothing of the kind. It is false pretense and false promise. It has served well in the past. Will it continue to catch the votes of unthinking and deluded workers?

What workingmen had part in the Republican national convention or were honored by it?

The grand coliseum swarmed with trust magnates, corporation barons, money lords, stock gamblers, professional politicians, lawyers, lobbyists and other plutocratic tools and mercenaries, but there was no room for the horny-handed and horny-headed sons of toil. They built it, but were not in it.

Compare that convention with the convention of the Socialist party, composed almost wholly of working men and women and controlled wholly in the interest of their class.

But a party is still better known by its chosen representatives than by its platform declarations.

Who are the nominees of the Republican party for the highest offices in the gift of the nation and what is their relation to the working class?

First of all, Theodore Roosevelt and Charles W. Fairbanks, candidates for President and Vice-President, respectively, deny the class struggle and this almost infallibly fixes their status as friends of capital and enemies of labor. They insist that they can serve both; but the fact is obvious that only one can be served and that one at the expense of the other. Mr. Roosevelt's whole political career proves it.

The capitalists made no mistake in nominating Mr. Roosevelt. They know him well and he has served them well. They know that his instincts, associations, tastes and desires are with them, that he is in fact one of them and that he has nothing in common with the working class.

The only evidence to the contrary is his membership in the Brotherhood of Locomotive Firemen which seems to have come to him co-incident with his ambition to succeed himself in the presidential chair. He is a full fledged member of the union, has the grip, signs and passwords; but it is not reported that he is attending meetings, doing picket duty, supporting strikes and boycotts and performing such other duties as his union obligation imposes.

When Ex-President Grover Cleveland violated the constitution and outraged justice by seizing the state of Illinois by the throat and handcuffing her civil administration at the behest of the crime-stained trusts and corporations, Theodore Roosevelt was among his most ardent admirers and enthusiastic supporters. He wrote in hearty commendation of the atrocious act, pronounced it most exalted patriotism and said he would have done the same himself had he been president.

And so he would and so he will!

How impressive to see the Rough Rider embrace the Smooth Statesman! Oyster Bay and Buzzard's Bay! "Two souls with but a single thought, two hearts that beat as one."

There is also the highest authority for the statement charging Mr. Roosevelt with declaring about the same time he was lauding Cleveland that if he was in command he would have such as Atgeld, Debs and other traitors lined up against a dead wall and shot. The brutal remark was not for publication but found its way into print and Mr. Roosevelt, after he became a candidate, attempted to make denial, but the words themselves sound like Roosevelt and bear the impress of his savage visage.

Following the Pullman strike in 1894 there was an indignant and emphatic popular protest against "government by injunction," which has not yet by any means subsided.

Organized labor was, and is, a unit against this insidious form of judicial usurpation as a means of abrogating constitutional restraints of despotic power.

Mr. Roosevelt with his usual zeal to serve the ruling class and keep their slaves in subjection, vaulted into the arena and launched his tirade upon the "mob" that dared oppose the divine rule of a corporation judge.

"Men who object to what they style 'government by injunctions,' " said he, "are, as regards the essential principles of government, in hearty sympathy with their remote skin-clad ancestors, who lived in caves, fought one another with stone-headed axes and ate the mammoth and woolly rhinoceros. They are dangerous whenever there is the least danger of their making the principles of this ages-buried past living factors in our present life. They are not in sympathy with men of good minds and good civic morality."

In direct terms and plain words Mr. Roosevelt denounces all those who oppose "Government by Injunction" as cannibals, barbarians and anarchists, and this violent and sweeping stigma embraces the whole organized movement of labor, every man, woman and child that wears the badge of union labor in the United States.

It is not strange in the light of these facts that the national congress, under President Roosevelt's administration, suppresses anti-injunction and eight-hour bills and all other measures favored by labor and resisted by capital.

No stronger or more convincing proof is required of Mr. Roosevelt's allegiance to capital and opposition to labor, nor of the class struggle and class rule which he so vehemently denies; and the workingman who in the face of these words and acts, can still support Mr. Roosevelt, must feel himself flattered in being publicly proclaimed a barbarian, and sheer gratitude, doubtless, impels him to crown his benefactors with the highest honors.

If the working class are barbarians, according to Mr. Roosevelt, this may account for his esteeming himself as having the very qualities necessary to make himself Chief of the Tribe.

But it must be noted that Mr. Roosevelt denounced organized labor as savages long before he was a candidate for president. After he became a candidate he joined the tribe and is today, himself, according to his own dictum, a barbarian and the enemy of civic morality.

The labor union to which President Roosevelt belongs and which he is solemnly obligated to support, is unanimously opposed to "Government by Injunction." President Roosevelt knew it when he joined it and he also knew that those who oppose injunction rule have the instincts of cannibals and are a menace to morality, but his proud nature succumbed to political ambition, and his ethical ideas vanished as he struck the trail that led to the tribe and, after a most dramatic scene and impressive ceremony, was decorated with the honorary badge of international barbarism.

How Theodore Roosevelt, the trade-unionist, can support the presidential candidate who denounced him as an immoral and dangerous barbarian, he may decide at his leisure, and so may all other union men in the United States who are branded with the same vulgar stigma, and their ballots will determine if they have the manhood to resent insult and rebuke its author, or if they have been fitly characterized and deserve humiliation and contempt.

The appointment of Judge Taft to a cabinet position is corroborative evidence, if any be required, of President Roosevelt's fervent faith in Government by Injunction. Judge Taft first came into national notoriety when, some years ago, sitting with Judge Ricks, who was later tried for malfeasance, they issued the celebrated injunction during the Toledo, Ann Arbor & North Michigan railroad strike that paralyzed the Brotherhood of Locomotive Engineers and Firemen and won for them the gratitude and esteem of every corporation in the land. They were hauled to Toledo, the headquarters of the railroad, in a special car, pulled by a special engine, on special time, and after hastily consulting the railroad magnates and receiving instructions, let go the judicial lightning that shivered the union to splinters and ended the strike in total defeat. Judge Taft is a special favorite with the trust barons and his elevation to the cabinet was ratified with joy at the court of St. Plutus.

Still again did President Roosevelt drive home his arch-enmity to labor and his implacable hostility to the trade-union movement when he made Paul Morton, the notorious union hater and union wrecker, his secretary of the navy. That appointment was an open insult to every trade-unionist in the country and they who lack the self-respect to resent it at the polls may wear the badge, but they are lacking wholly in the spirit and principles of union labor.

Go ask the brotherhood men who were driven from the C. B. & Q. and the striking union machinists on the Santa Fe to give you the pedigree of Mr. Morton and you will learn that his hate for union men is equaled only by his love for the scabs who take their places.

Such a man and such another as Sherman Bell, the military ferret of the Colorado mine owners, are the ideal patriots and personal chums of Mr. Roosevelt, and by honoring these he dishonors himself and should be repudiated by the ballot of every working man in the nation.

Mr. Fairbanks, the Republican candidate for Vice-President, is a corporation attorney of the first class and a plutocrat in good and regular standing. He is in every respect a fit and proper representative of his party and every millionaire in the land may safely support him.

THE DEMOCRATIC PARTY

In referring to the Democratic party in this discussion we may save time by simply saying that since it was born again at the St. Louis convention it is near enough like its Republican ally to pass for a twin brother.

The former party of the "common people" is no longer under the boycott of the plutocracy since it has adopted the Wall street label and renounced its middle class heresies.

The radical and progressive elements of the former Democracy have been evicted and must seek other quarters. They were an unmitigated nuisance in the conservative counsels of the old party. They were for the "common people" and the trusts have no use for such a party.

Where but to the Socialist party can these progressive people turn? They are now without a party and the only genuine democratic party in the field is the Socialist party, and every true Democrat should thank Wall street for driving him out of a party that is democratic in name only and into one that is democratic in fact.

The St. Louis convention was a trust jubilee. The Wall street reorganizers made short work of the free silver element. From first to last it was a capitalistic convocation. Labor was totally ignored. As an incident, two thousand choice chairs were reserved for the Business Men's League of St. Louis, an organization hostile to organized labor, but not a chair was tendered to those whose labor had built the convention hall, had clothed, transported, fed and wined the delegates and whose votes are counted on as if they were so many dumb driven cattle, to pull the ticket through in November.

As another incident, when Lieutenant Richmond Hobson dramatically declared that President Cleveland had been the only president who had ever been patriotic enough to use the federal troops to crush union labor, the trust agents, lobbyists, tools and clackers screamed with delight and the convention shook with applause.

The platform is precisely the same as the Republican platform in relation to labor. It says nothing and means the same. A plank was proposed condemning the outrages in Colorado under Republican administration, but upon order from the Parryites it was promptly thrown aside.

The editor of *American Industries*, organ of the Manufacturers Association, condemned at length in its issue of July 15 on the triumph of capital and the defeat of labor at both Republican and Democratic national conventions. Among other things he said: "The two labor lobbies, partly similar in make-up, were, to put it bluntly, thrown out bodily in both places." And that is the simple fact and is known of all men who read the papers. The capitalist organs exult because labor, to use their own brutal expression, was kicked bodily out of both the Republican and Democratic national conventions.

What more than this is needed to open the eyes of workingmen to the fact that neither of these parties is their party and that they are as strangely out of place in them as Rockefeller and Vanderbilt would be in the Socialist party?

And how many more times are they to be "kicked out bodily" before they stay out and join the party of their class in which labor is not only honored but is supreme, a party that is clean, that has conscience and convictions, a party that will one day sweep the old parties from the field like chaff and issue the Proclamation of Labor's Emancipation?

Judge Alton B. Parker corresponds precisely to the Democratic platform. It was made to order for him. His famous telegram in the expiring hour removed the last wrinkle and left it a perfect fit.

Thomas W. Lawson, the Boston millionaire, charges that Senator Patrick McCarren, who brought out Judge Parker for the nomination, is on the pay roll of the Standard Oil Company as political master mechanic at twenty thousand dollars a year, and that Parker is the chosen tool of Standard Oil. Mr. Lawson offers Senator McCarren one hundred thousand dollars if he will disprove the charge.

William Jennings Bryan denounced Judge Parker as a tool of Wall street before he was nominated and declared that no self-respecting Democrat could vote for him, and after his nomination he charged that it had been dictated by the trusts and secured by "crooked and indefensible methods." Mr. Bryan also said that labor had been betrayed in the convention and need look for nothing from the Democratic party. He made many other damaging charges against his party and its candidates, but when the supreme test came he was not equal to it, and instead of denouncing the betrayers of the "common people" and repudiating their made-to-order Wall street program, he compromised with the pirates that scuttled his ship and promised with his lips the support his heart refused and his conscience condemned.

The Democratic nominee for President was one of the Supreme Judges of the State of New York who declared the eight-hour law unconstitutional and this is an index of his political character.

In his address accepting the nomination he makes but a single allusion to labor and in this he takes occasion to say that labor is charged with having recently used dynamite in destroying property and that the perpetrators should be subjected to "the most rigorous punishment known to the law." This cruel intimation amounts to conviction in advance of trial and indicates clearly the trend of his capitalistically trained judicial mind. He made no such reference to capital, nor to those ermined rascals who use judicial dynamite in blowing up the constitution while labor is looted and starved by capitalistic freebooters who trample all law in the mire and leer and mock at their despoiled and helpless victims.

It is hardly necessary to make more than passing reference to Henry G. Davis, Democratic candidate for Vice-President. He is a coal baron, railroad owner and, of course, an enemy to union labor. He has amassed a great fortune exploiting his wage-slaves and has always strenuously resisted every attempt to organize them for the betterment of their condition. Mr. Davis is a staunch believer in the virtue of the injunction as applied to union labor. As a young man he was in charge of a slave plantation and his conviction is that wage-slaves should be kept free from the contaminating influence of the labor agitator and render cheerful obedience to their master.

Mr. Davis is as well qualified to serve his party as is Senator Fairbanks to serve the Republican party and wage-workers should have no trouble in making their choice between this pernicious pair of plutocrats, and certainly no intelligent workingman will hesitate an instant to discard them both and cast his vote for Ben Hanford, their working class competitor, who is as loyally devoted to labor as Fairbanks and Davis are to capital.

THE SOCIALIST PARTY

In what has been said of other parties I have tried to show why they should not be supported by the common people, least of all by workingmen, and I think I have shown clearly enough that such workers as do support them are guilty, consciously or unconsciously, of treason to their class. They are voting into power the enemies of labor and are morally responsible for the crimes thus perpetrated upon their fellow-workers, and sooner or later they will have to suffer the consequences of their miserable acts.

The Socialist party is not, and does not pretend to be, a capitalist party. It does not ask, nor does it expect, the votes of the capitalist class. Such capitalists as do support it do so seeing the approaching doom of the capitalist system and with a full understanding that the Socialist party is not a capitalist party, nor a middle class party, but a revolutionary working class party, whose historic mission it is to conquer capitalism on the political battle-field, take control of government and through the public powers take possession of the means of wealth production, abolish wage-slavery and emancipate all workers and all humanity.

The people are as capable of achieving their industrial freedom as they were to secure their political liberty, and both are necessary to a free nation.

The capitalist system is no longer adapted to the needs of modern society. It is outgrown and fetters the forces of progress. Industrial and commercial competition are largely of the past. The handwriting blazes on the wall. Centralization and combination are the modern forces in industrial and commercial life. Competition is breaking down and co-operation is supplanting it.

The hand tools of early times are used no more. Mammoth machines have taken their place. A few thousand capitalists own them and many millions of workingmen use them.

All the wealth the vast army of labor produces above its subsistence is taken by the machine owning capitalists, who also own the land and the mills, the factories, railroads and mines, the forests and fields and all other means of transportation.

Hence wealth and poverty, millionaires and beggars, castles and caves, luxury and squalor, painted parasites on the boulevard and painted poverty among the red lights.

Hence strikes, boycotts, riots, murder, suicide, insanity, prostitution on a fearful and increasing scale.

The capitalist parties can do nothing. They are a part, an iniquitous part, of the foul and decaying system.

There is no remedy for the ravages of death.

Capitalism is dying and its extremities are already decomposing. The blotches upon the surface show that the blood no longer circulates. The time is near when the cadaver will have to be removed and the atmosphere purified.

In contrast with the Republican and Democratic conventions, where politicians were the puppets of plutocrats, the convention of the Socialist party consisted of workingmen and women fresh from the labors, strong, clean, wholesome, self-reliant, ready to do and dare for the cause of labor, the cause of humanity.

Proud indeed am I to have been chosen by such a body of men and women to bear aloft the proletarian standard in this campaign, and heartily do I endorse the clear and cogent platform of the party which appeals with increasing force and eloquence to the whole working class of the country.

To my associate upon the national ticket I give my hand with all my heart. Ben Hanford typifies the working class and fitly represents the historic mission and revolutionary character of the Socialist party.

CLOSING WORDS

These are stirring days for living men. The day of crisis is drawing near and Socialists are exerting all their power to prepare the people for it.

The old order of society can survive but little longer. Socialism is next in order. The swelling minority sounds warning of the impending change. Soon that minority will be the majority and then will come the co-operative commonwealth.

Every workingman should rally to the standard of his class and hasten the full-orbed day of freedom.

Every progressive Democrat must find his way in our direction and if he will but free himself from prejudice and study the principles of Socialism he will soon be a sturdy supporter of our party.

Every sympathizer with labor, every friend of justice, every lover of humanity should support the Socialist party as the only party that is organized to abolish industrial slavery, the prolific source of the giant evils that afflict the people.

Who with a heart in his breast can look upon Colorado without keenly feeling the cruelties and crimes of capitalism! Repression will not help her. Brutality will only brutalize her. Private ownership and wage-slavery are the curse of Colorado. Only Socialism will save Colorado and the nation.

The overthrow of capitalism is the object of the Socialist party. It will not fuse with any other party and it would rather die than compromise.

The Socialist party comprehends the magnitude of its task and has the patience of preliminary defeat and the faith of ultimate victory.

The working class must be emancipated by the working class.

Woman must be given her true place in society by the working class.

Child labor must be abolished by the working class.

Society must be reconstructed by the working class.

The working class must be employed by the working class.

The fruits of labor must be enjoyed by the working class.

War, bloody war, must be ended by the working class.

These are the principles and objects of the Socialist party and we fearlessly proclaim them to our fellowmen.

We know our cause is just and that it must prevail.

With faith and hope and courage we hold our heads erect and with dauntless spirit marshal the working class for the march from Capitalism to Socialism, from Slavery to Freedom, from Barbarism to Civilization.

The Coming Union

Daily People, Vol. VI, No. 123. Tuesday, October 31, 1905.

The opponents of the Industrial Workers, numerous, varied and powerful though they be, will find themselves baffled in every attempt they make to stem the tide of new industrial organization.

These opponents, strange as it may seem, embrace, besides the capitalist class and their "labor lieutenants," Socialists who profess to favor industrial unionism and trades unionists who profess to be class conscious workingmen!

An anomalous situation, indeed!

The only national labor union that recognizes the class struggle, the Industrial Workers of the World, is opposed, and the American Federation of labor, whose leaders deny the class struggle, is supported by men who call themselves Socialists and class conscious workingmen.

But in spite of all this the Industrial Workers is the coming labor union in the United States and all the powers of capitalism and all the resources of its emissaries cannot prevent it.

The conditions are mature for it and the working class will embrace it and stand by it as they learn to comprehend its meaning and grasp its mission.

Three years ago, when the Western Federation of Miners and the American Labor Union, in national convention assembled, in Denver, struck the new trail of class-consciousness and declared in favor of independent political action along working class lines, the very thing Socialists have been clamoring for, the press of the Socialist party, almost solidly, instead of cheering the new departure and encouraging and supporting the movement, treated the matter coldly, or damned it with faint praise.

These papers felt themselves committed to the American Federation of Labor and feared to offend the anti-Socialist organization. Upon no other ground is such opposition to Socialist action by Socialist papers conceivable.

When the Industrial Workers of the World was recently organized at Chicago the same Socialist papers fought the movement openly, or, what revealed the same antagonistic attitude, remained silent.

These Socialist papers, smiling patronizingly upon the American Federation of Labor which repudiates and despises them, and frowning scornfully upon the Industrial Workers of the World, a truly class-conscious organization, have committed a grave mistake and appearances indicate they are beginning to realize it. The open opposition has died out and silence has taken its place. They have evidently heard from the rank and file. In any event it may be well for them to know that De Leon's *Weekly People* is getting a harvest of new subscribers, including many members of our party, because of his espousal of the Industrial Workers.

That Socialists can still find it consistent to remain in the American Federation of Labor in the light of its fixed procapitalist policy is, I confess, incomprehensible to me.

Why do they not apply their peculiar logic to the political situation? The Republican and Democratic parties both consist mainly of workingmen. Why not turn them into working class parties? The workingmen have a majority in both—why organize a Socialist party?

The workingman who reasons in that way and attends Republican and Democratic conventions as a delegate is by Socialists set down as ignoramus or fakir, and yet that is precisely the attitude of certain Socialists with reference to the old anti-labor federation and the new working class union.

The American Federation of Labor, which is simply an attempt to harmonize pure and simple trade unions, that were built up on tools long since discarded and on principles long out of date, is the enemy of working class solidarity. It is in the control of the capitalist class. The Civic Federation and its personnel is sufficient proof of this fact.

It leers at the class struggle.

Professing to oppose independent political action by the working class and even forbidding the discussion of political questions, it connives with the political hucksters of capitalist parties in consideration of beggarly "hand-outs" for its henchmen.

This aggregation of one time labor organizations have veered about and are now thoroughly reactionary, and every inch of genuine working class progress from this time forward will have to be made in spite of them.

Would but Socialists remain away from the national convention of this alleged federation the jurisdictional lightnings would then have full play and soon strike and sever the flimsy bonds that hold the old antiquated unions together. The few Socialists serve the federation leaders in the valuable role of lightning rods to attract and divert the bolts of disintegration. These Socialist comrades are on a cold trail. Their misguided zeal is worthy of a better cause. There was a time when their efforts bore fruit, but that day is passed. They might as well spend their time, as Thomas Paine put it, "administering medicine to a corpse." The role they are now in at the federation convention is almost pathetic. Even the applause in the gallery is dying out. They are sadly out of place. They are in truth laughing stock—the footballs of two by four fakirs that serve the capitalist class for their stereotyped dispatch reporting the annual kicking out of Socialism by the American Federation of Labor.

When the moon turns into green cheese will these Socialists succeed in converting the American Federation of Labor, honey-combed with capitalistic influences, into a revolutionary working class organization.

But in the meantime they are extremely valuable to the federation leaders, who would undoubtedly seriously regret to be deprived of their services.

The opposition to the Industrial Workers inspired by personal hatred for Daniel De Leon and the Socialist Trade & Labor Alliance is puerile, to say the least. With all that has been said about the latter it has never been charged with being a capitalist annex and as for De Leon personally he is not an issue to be considered when choosing between a bona-fide labor union organization for the benefit of the working class and a bogus labor organization defended by every capitalist paper and supported by every capitalist politician in the land.

De Leon is sound on the question of trade unionism and to that extent, whether I like him or not personally, I am with him.

My personal likes and dislikes are secondary to my allegiance to the working class.

The choice is between the A. F. of L. and capitalism on one side and the Industrial Workers of the World and Socialism on the other.

The A. F. of L. is for the wages system; the Industrial Workers of the World for its abolition.

How can a Socialist hesitate in his choice an instant?

The A. F. of L. keeps the working class divided into trades which have ceased to exist; the Industrial Workers unites them into one compact militant body.

Which of these truly expresses the present industrial situation and which actually stands for working class solidarity?

As a member of both the Industrial Workers and the Socialist party I want to see one class-conscious labor union on the industrial field and one class-conscious labor party on the political field, each the counterpart of the other, and both working together in harmonious co-operation to overthrow the capitalist system and emancipate the workers from wage slavery.

The Industrial Workers has made a sound beginning and at its convention the work will be rounded out and the organization fairly started on its mission of proletarian emancipation.

The time has come to strike out boldly and cut loose from all associations that are not with and for the revolutionary program of the working class. Any professed labor organization that does not recognize the class struggle and stand squarely on the right side of it forfeits all claim to the respect of intelligent workingmen; and to remain with it is not to help the union get right, but to risk personal contamination.

The way to serve the working class through the A. F. of L. is to get out of it and leave the capitalist class and their henchmen in undisputed control.

The paramount question is the labor movement and working class victory. All other things—parties and unions included—are secondary.

Therefore, organization, economic and political, along class lines. Any organization that attempts to obscure these lines damns itself.

The Industrial Workers is right. It has come at the right time and it will fight its way to the front! It is asking no favors of capitalism and granting none; it is pandering to no organization and no man or set of men to curry favors; it stands squarely on the class struggle, defiantly challenging the capitalist class, relying only upon the awakening working class to rally to its standard and carry it to victory.

Revolutionary Unionism

Speech at Chicago, November 25, 1905.

The unity of labor, economic and political, upon the basis of the class struggle, is at this time the supreme need of the working class. The prevailing lack of unity implies lack of class consciousness; that is to say, enlightened self-interest; and this can, must and will be overcome by revolutionary education and organization. Experience, long, painful and dearly bought, has taught some of us that craft division is fatal to class unity. To accomplish its mission the working class must be united. They must act together; they must assert their combined power, and when they do this upon the basis of the class struggle, then and then only will they break the fetters of wage slavery.

We are engaged today in a class war; and why? For the simple reason that in the evolution of the capitalist system in which we live, society has been mainly divided into two economic classes—a small class of capitalists who own the tools with which work is done and wealth is produced, and a great mass of workers who are compelled to use those tools. Between these two classes there is an irrepressible economic conflict. Unfortunately for himself, the workingman does not yet understand the nature of the conflict, and for this reason has hitherto failed to accomplish any effective unity of his class.

It is true that workers in the various departments of industrial activity have organized trade unions. It is also true that in this capacity they have from time to time asserted such power as this form of organization has conferred upon them. It is equally true that mere craft unionism, no matter how well it may be organized, is in the present highly developed capitalist system utterly unable to successfully cope with the capitalist class. The old craft union has done its work and belongs to the past. Labor unionism, like everything else, must recognize and bow to the inexorable law of evolution.

The craft union says that the worker shall receive a fair day's pay for a fair day's work. What is a fair day's pay for a fair day's work? Ask the capitalist and he will give you his idea about it. Ask the worker and, if he is intelligent, he will tell you that a fair day's pay for a fair day's work is all the workingman produces.

While the craft unionist still talks about a fair day's pay for a fair day's work, implying that the economic interests of the capitalist and the worker can be harmonized upon a basis of equal justice to both, the Industrial Worker says, "I want all I produce by my labor."

If the worker is not entitled to all he produces, then what share is anybody else entitled to?

Does the worker today receive all he produces? Does he receive anything like a fair (?) share of the product of his labor? Will any trade-unionist of the old school make any such claim, and if he is bold enough to make it, can he verify it?

The student of this question knows that, as a matter of fact, in the capitalist system in which we live today the worker who produces all wealth receives but enough of his product to keep him in working and producing order. His wage, in the aggregate, is fixed by his living necessities. It suffices, upon the average, to maintain him according to the prevailing standard of living and to enable him to reproduce himself in the form of labor power. He receives, as a matter of fact, but about 17 per cent of what his labor produces.

The worker produces a certain thing. It goes from the manufacturer to the jobber, from the jobber to the wholesaler, and from the wholesaler to the retailer—each of these adding a profit, and when it completes the circle and comes back to the worker who produced it and he stands face to face with the product of his own labor, he can buy back, upon the average, with his paltry wage but about 17 per cent of it. In other words, he is exploited, robbed, of about 83 per cent of what his labor produces. And why? For the simple reason that in modern industry, the tool, in the form of a great machine with which he works and produces, is the private property of the capitalist, who didn't make it, and could not, if his life depended upon it, use it.

The evolution is not yet complete.

By virtue of his private ownership of the social tool—made and used by the co-operative labor of the working class—the employer has the economic power to appropriate to himself, as a capitalist, what is produced by the social labor of the working class. This accounts for the fact that the capitalist becomes fabulously rich, lives in a palace where there is music and singing and dancing, and where there is the luxury of all climes, while the workingmen who do the work and produce the wealth and endure the privations and make the sacrifices of health and limb and life, remain in a wretched state of poverty and dependence.

The exploiting capitalist is the economic master and the political ruler in capitalist society, and as such holds the exploited wage worker in utter contempt.

No master ever had any respect for his slave, and no slave ever had, or ever could have, any real love for his master.

I must beg you to indulge the hoarseness of my voice, which has been somewhat strained addressing meetings of the Industrial Workers held in and about Chicago during the last two or three evenings; but, fortunately, my eyesight has not been strained reading the accounts of these meetings in the capitalist papers of Chicago.

Alert, vigilant, argus-eyed as the capitalist dailies of Chicago are, there is not one of them that knows of this meeting of the Industrial Workers. But if this were a meeting of the American Federation of Labor and an old trade union leader were here, you would read tomorrow morning a full account of it and him in every capitalist paper in the city. There is a reason for this that explains itself.

The capitalist papers know that there is such an organization as the Industrial Workers, because they have lied about it. Just now they are ignoring it. Let me serve notice on them through you and the thousands of others who flock to our meetings everywhere, that they will reckon with the Industrial Workers before six months have rolled around.

There are those wage workers who feel their economic dependence, who know that the capitalist for whom they work is the owner of their job, and therefore the master of their fate, who are still vainly seeking by individual effort and through waning craft unions to harmonize the conflicting interests of the exploiting capitalist and the exploited wage slave. They are engaged in a vain and hopeless task. They are wasting time and energy worthy of a better cause. These interests never can and never will be harmonized permanently, and when they are adjusted even temporarily it is always at the expense of the working class.

It is no part of the mission of this revolutionary working class union to conciliate the capitalist class. We are organized to fight that class, and we want that class to distinctly understand it. And they do understand it, and in time the working class will also understand it; and then the capitalist class will have reason to understand it better still. Their newspapers understand it so well even now that they have not a single favorable comment to make upon it.

When the convention of delegates was in session here in June last for the purpose of organizing the Industrial Workers, every report that appeared in a Chicago paper—capitalist paper I mean; every single report was a tissue of perversion, misstatement and downright falsehood. They knew that we had met for a purpose, and that that purpose was to fight the class of which they are the official mouthpieces. Now, it seems to me that this uniform hostility of the capitalist press ought to be significant to even the unthinking workingman. Capitalist papers are, as a rule, quite friendly to the craft unions. They do not misrepresent them; do no lie about them; do not traduce their representatives. They are exceedingly fond of them, because they know enough about their own interests to know that the craft unions are not only not a menace to them, but are in fact bulwarks of defense to them. And why? Because, chiefly, craft unions divide and do not unite the working class. And I challenge contradiction.

There was a time when the craft union expressed in terms of unionism the prevailing mode of industry. That was long ago when production was still mainly carried on by handicraftsmen with hand tools; when one man worked for another to learn his trade that he might become its master. The various trades involved skill and cunning; considerable time was required to master them. This was in the early stages of the capitalist system. Even at that early day the antagonism between employer and employed found expression, although the employer was not at that time the capitalist as he is today. The men who followed these trades found it necessary in order to protect themselves in their trade interests to band together, form a union, so that they might act together in resisting the encroachments of the "boss." So the trade union came into existence.

The mode of production since that time has been practically revolutionized. The hand tool has all but disappeared. The mammoth machine has taken its place. The hand tool was made and used by the individual worker and was largely within his own control. Today the machine that has supplanted the old tool is not owned nor controlled by the man, or rather the men, who use it. As I have already said, it is the private property of some capitalist who may live at a remote point and never have seen the machine or the wage slaves who operate it.

In other words, the production of wealth, in the evolution of industry, from being an individual act a half century ago has become a social act. The tool, from being an individual tool, has become a social instrument. So that the tool has been socialized and production has also been socialized. But the evolution is yet to complete its work. This social tool, made socially and used socially, must be socially owned.

In the evolution of industry the trade has been largely undermined. The old trade union expresses the old form of industry, the old mode of individual production based upon the use of the individual tool. That tool has about disappeared; that mode of production has also about disappeared, but the trade union built upon that mode of production, springing from the use of the hand tool, remains essentially the same.

The pure and simple trade union, in seeking to preserve its autonomy, is forced into conflict with other trade unions by the unceasing operation of the laws of industrial evolution. How many of the skilled trades that were in operation half a century ago are still practiced?

At the town where I live there used to be quite a number of cooper shops. Barrels were made by hand and a cooper shop consisted wholly of coopers. The coopers' union was organized and served fairly well the purposes of the coopers of that day, but it does not serve the purposes of the workers who make barrels today. They do not make barrels in the way they used to be made. Today we want a union that expresses the economic interests of all the workers in the cooperage plant engaged in making and handling barrels. But a few coopers still remain, a very few. It is no longer necessary to be a cooper to make a barrel. The machine is the cooper today. The machine makes the barrel, and almost anyone can operate the machine that makes the barrel.

You will observe that labor has been subdivided and specialized and that the trade has been dissipated; and now a body of men and boys work together co-operatively in the making of a barrel, each making a small part of a barrel. Now we want a union which embraces all the workers engaged in making barrels. We lose sight of the cooper trade as evolution has practically disposed of that. We say that since the trade has completely changed, the union which expressed that trade must also change accordingly. In the new union we shall include not only the men who are actually engaged in the making of barrels directly, but also those who are placing them upon the market. There are the typewriters, the bookkeepers, the teamsters, and all other classes of labor that are involved in the making and delivering of the barrels. We insist that all the workers in the whole of any given plant shall belong to one and the same union.

This is the very thing the workers need and the capitalist who owns the establishment does not want. He believes in labor unionism if it is the "right kind." And if it is the right kind for him it is the wrong kind for you. He is more than willing that his employers shall join the craft union. He has not the slightest objection. On the contrary, it is easily proven that capitalists are among the most active upholders of the old craft unions.

The capitalists are perfectly willing that you shall organize, as long as you don't do a thing against them; as long as you don't do a thing for yourselves. You cannot do a thing for yourselves without antagonizing them; and you don't antagonize them through your craft unions nearly as much as you buttress their interests and prolong their mastery.

The average workingman imagines that he must have a leader to look to; a guide to follow, right or wrong. He has been taught in the craft union that he is a very dependent creature; that without a leader the goblins would get him without a doubt, and he therefore instinctively looks to his leader. And even while he is looking at his leader there is someone else looking at the same leader from the other side.

You have depended too much on that leader and not enough on yourself. I don't want you to follow me. I want you to cultivate self-reliance.

If I have the slightest capacity for leadership I can only give evidence of it by leading you to rely upon yourselves.

As long as you can be led by an individual you will be betrayed by an individual. That does not mean that all leaders are dishonest or corrupt. I make no such sweeping indictment. I know that many of them are honest. I know also that many of them are in darkness themselves, blind leaders of the blind. That is the worst that can be said of them. And let me say to you that the most dangerous leader is not the corrupt leader, but the honest, ignorant leader. That leader is just as fatal to your interests as the one who deliberately sells you out for a paltry consideration.

You are a workingman! Now, at your earliest leisure look yourself over and take an inventory of your resources. Invoice your mental stock; see what you have on hand.

You may be of limited mentality; and that is all you require in the capitalist system. You need only small brains, but huge hands.

Most of your hands are calloused and you are taught by the capitalist politician, who is the political mercenary of the capitalist who fleeces you, you are taught by him to be proud of your horny hands. If that is true he ought to be ashamed of his.

He doesn't have any horns on his hands. He has them on his brain. He is as busy with his brain as you are with your hands, and because he is busy with his brain and you neglect yours, he gets a goodly share of what you produce with your hands. He is the gentleman who calls you the horny handed sons of toil. That fetches you every time. I tell you that the time has come for you to use your brains in your own interest, and until you do that you will have to use your hands in the interest of your masters.

Now, after you have looked yourself over; after you have satisfied yourself what you are, or rather, what you are not, you will arrive at the conclusion that as a wage worker in capitalist society you are not a man at all. You are simply a thing. And that thing is bought in the labor market, just as hair, hides and other forms of merchandise are bought.

When the capitalist requires the use of your hands, does he call for men? Why, certainly not. He doesn't want men, he only wants hands. And when he calls for hands, that is what he wants. Have you ever seen a placard posted: "Fifty hands wanted"? Did you ever know of a capitalist to respond to that kind of an invitation?

President Roosevelt would have you believe that there are no classes in the United States. He was made President by the votes of the working class. Did you ever know of his stopping over night in the home of a workingman? Is it by mere chance that he is always sheltered beneath the hospitable roof of some plutocrat? Not long ago he made a visit here and he gave a committee representing the workers about fifteen minutes of his precious time, just time enough to rebuke them with the intimation that organized labor consisted of a set of law-breakers, and then he gave fifteen hours to the plutocrats of Chicago, being wined and dined by them to prove that there are no classes in the United States, and that you, horny handed veteran, with your wage of $1.50 a day, with six children to support on that, are in the same class with John D. Rockefeller! Your misfortune is that you do not know you are in the same class. But on election day it dawns upon you and you prove it by voting the same ticket.

Since you have looked yourself over thoroughly, you realize by this time that, as a workingman, you have been supporting, through your craft unions and through your ballots, a social system that is the negation of your manhood.

The capitalist for whom you work doesn't have to go out and look for you; you have to look for him, and you belong to him just as completely as if he had a title to your body; as if you were his chattel slave.

He doesn't own you under law, but he does under the fact.

Why? Because he owns the tool with which you work, and you have got to have access to that tool if you work; and if you want to live you have got to work. If you don't work you don't eat; and so, scourged by hunger pangs, you look about for that tool and you locate it, and you soon discover that between yourself, a workingman, and that tool that is an essential part of yourself in industry, there stands the capitalist who owns it. He is your boss; he owns your job, takes your product and controls your destiny. Before you can touch that tool to earn a dime you must petition the owner of it to allow you to use it, in consideration of your giving to him all you produce with it, except just enough to keep you alive and in working order.

Observe that you are displaced by the surplus product of your own labor; that what you produce is of more value under capitalism than you who produce it; that the commodity which is the result of your labor is of greater value under capitalism than your own life. You consist of palpitating flesh; you have wants. You have necessities. You cannot satisfy them, and you suffer. But the product of your labor, the property of the capitalist — that is sacred; that must be protected at all hazards. After you have been displaced by the surplus product of your labor and you have been idle long enough, you become restive and you begin to speak out, and you become a menace. The unrest culminates in trouble. The capitalist presses a button and the police are called into action. Then the capitalist presses button No. 2 and injunctions are issued by the judges, the judicial allies and servants of the capitalist class. Then button No. 3 is pressed and the state troops fall into line; and if this is not sufficient button No. 4 is pressed and the regular soldiers come marching to the scene. That is what President Roosevelt meant when he said that back of the mayor is the governor, back of the governor the President; or, to use his own words, back of the city, the state and back of the state the nation—the capitalist nation.

If you have been working in a steel mill and you have made more steel than your master can sell, and you are locked out and get hungry, and the soldiers are called out, it is to protect the steel and shoot you who made the steel—to guard the men who steal the steel and kill the men who made it.

I am not asking you to withdraw from the craft unions simply because the Industrial Workers has been formed. I am asking you to think about these matters for yourselves.

I belonged to a craft union from the time I was nineteen years of age. I can remember the very evening I first joined the Brotherhood of Locomotive Firemen. I can recall with what zeal I went to work to organize my craft, and it was the pride of my life to see that union expand. I did what I could to build it up. In time I was made to realize that that union was not sufficient unto itself. I next did what I could to organize other branches of the service and then establish a federation of the various unions of railroad employees, and finally succeeded; but soon after the federation was formed, on account of craft jealousies, it was disrupted. I then, along with a number of others who had had the same experience and had profited by it, undertook to organize the railway men within one organization, known as the American Railway Union. The railroad corporations were the deadly enemies of that organization. They understood that its purpose was to unify all the railroad employees. They knew that the unity of the working class meant their end, and so they set their faces like flint against the American Railway Union.

And while they were using all their powers to crush and to stamp out the American Railway Union, they were bestowing all their favors upon the several craft brotherhoods, the engineers and the firemen, the conductors and the brakemen. They knew that so long as these craft unions existed there could be no unification of the men employed in the railway service.

Are the railroad men of this country organized today? No! Not nearly one-half of them are organized at all. And when the railroad corporations from motives of good policy make a concession to the engineers of the conductors, it is gouged out of the poor devils who work for a dollar a day and are compelled to submit.

There are a great many engineers who are perfectly willing to be tied up in a contract. They think they can save themselves at the expense of their fellow-workers. But they are going to reap, sooner or later, just what they have sown. In the next few years they will become motormen.

While we are upon this question, let us consult industrial history a moment. We will begin with the craft union railroad strike of 1888. The Brotherhood of Engineers and the Brotherhood of Firemen on the C., B. & Q. system went out on strike. Some 2,000 engineers and firemen vacated their posts and went out on one of the most bitterly contested railroad, the rest of the employees, especially the conductors, who were organized in craft unions of their own, remained at their posts, and the union conductors piloted the scab engineers over the line. I know whereof I speak. I was there. I took an active part in that strike.

I saw craft union pitted against craft union, and I saw the Brotherhood of Engineers and the Brotherhood of Firemen completely wiped from the C.,B. & Q. system. And now you find these men, seventeen years later, scattered all over the United States. They had to pay the penalty of their ignorance in organizing a craft instead of organizing as a whole.

In 1892 a strike occurred on the Lehigh Valley; the same result. Another on the Toledo, Ann Arbor & North Michigan. Same result. The engineers have had no strike from that time to this. Every time they have had a strike they have been defeated.

The railroad corporations are shrewd enough to recognize the fact that if they can keep certain departments in their employ in a time of emergency they can defeat all the rest. A manager of a railroad who can keep control of 15 per cent of the old men can allow 85 per cent to go out on strike and defeat them every time. That is why they have made some concessions to the engineers and conductors and brakemen, and now and then to the switchmen, the most militant labor union of them all.

A year and a half ago the telegraph operators on the Missouri, Kansas & Texas went out on strike. The engineer remained at his post; so did the fireman; the conductor at his; and the brakeman at his. And they hauled the scabs that flocked from all parts of the country to the several points along the line, and delivered them in good order to take the places vacated by the strikers; worked all round them and with them until they had mastered the details of their several duties; and having done this, the strike was at an end, and the 1,300 craft unionists out of jobs. You will find them scattered all over the country.

Now, were not these other craft unions scabbing on the telegraphers just as flagrantly as if they had stepped into their positions and discharged their duties? They were acting with the corporation against their union fellow workingmen, helping the corporation to defeat and crush them. Without their aid the corporation could not have succeeded. With their aid it was very easily done.

Is it possible that a craft unionist can see such an object lesson as this so plainly presented to him and still refuse to profit by it? Still close his eyes and, as it were, shut up his reason, and absolutely decline to see that this is suicidal policy and that its fruit must always be disruption and disaster?

This world only respects as it is compelled to respect; and if you workingmen would be respected you must begin by respecting yourselves. You have had enough of this sort of experience. You have had more than enough of it right here in Chicago.

Why didn't the steel trust annihilate the Amalgamated Steelworkers? Only two years ago they defeated them completely. The trust had its iron heel upon the neck of the Steelworkers Union, and could have, had it chosen, completely crushed the life out of it. But Morgan was too wily. Schwab was too wise. They used to oppose trade unions. They don't oppose them any longer. They have discovered that a union can be turned the other way; that it can be made useful to them instead of being useful to the working class. Morgan now says he is in favor of trade unions, and Schwab agrees. They didn't crush out the Steelworkers' Union because they knew that another and a better one would spring from its ruins. They were perfectly willing that the old craft union should grow up again and block the way to real union.

You have had a machinists strike here in Chicago. You are well aware of this without my telling you. There is something pathetic to me about every strike.

I have said and say again that no strike was ever lost; that it has always been worth all it cost. An essential part of a workingman's education is the defeats he encounters. The strikes he loses are after all the only ones he wins. I am heartily glad for myself that I lost the strike. It is the best thing that ever happened to me. I lost the strike of the past that I may win the strike of the future.

I am a discredited labor leader, but I have good staying qualities. The very moment the capitalist press credits me with being a wise labor leader, I will invite you to investigate me upon the charge of treason. I am discredited by the capitalist simply because I am true to his victim. I don't want his favors. I do not court his approbation. I would not have it. I can't afford it. If I had his respect it would be at the price of my own.

I don't care anything about what is called public opinion. I know precisely what that means. It is but the reflect of the interests of the capitalist class. As between the respect of the public and my own, I prefer my own; and I am going to keep it until I can have both.

When I pick up a capitalist newspaper and read a eulogy of some labor leader, I know that that leader has at least two afflictions; the one is mental weakness and the other is moral cowardice—and they go together. Put it down that when the capitalist who is exploiting you credits your leader with being safe and conservative and wise, that leader is not serving you. And if you take exception to that statement, just ask me to prove it.

The rank and file of all unions, barring their ignorance, are all right. The working class as a whole is all right. Many of them are misguided, and stand in the light of their own interest.

It is sometimes necessary that we offend you and even shock you, that you may understand that we are your friends and not your enemies. And if we are against your unions it is because we are for you. We know that you have paid your dues into them for years and that you are animated by a spirit of misdirected loyalty to those unions.

I can remember that it was not a very easy matter for me to give up the union in which I had spent my boyhood and all the years of my young manhood. I remember that I felt there was something in it in the nature of a sacrifice, and yet I had to make it in the nature of a sacrifice, and yet I had to make it in the interest of the larger duty that I owned myself and the working class.

Let me say to you, if you are a craft unionist, that infinitely greater than your loyalty to you craft is your loyalty to the working class as a whole. No craft union can fight this great battle successfully alone. The craft is a part, a part only, of the great body of the working class. And the time has come for his class, numerically overwhelming in the majority, to follow in one respect at least the example of its capitalist masters and unite as whole.

In this barbarous competitive struggle in which we are engaged, the workers, the millions, are fighting each other to sell themselves into slavery; the middle class are fighting each other to other to get enough trade to keep soul and body together, and the professional class are fighting each other like savages for practice. And this is called civilization! What a mockery! What a sham! There is no real civilization in the capitalist system.

Today there is nothing so easily produced as wealth. The whole earth consists of raw materials; and in every breath of nature, in sunshine, and in shower, hidden everywhere, are the subtle forces that may, by the touch of the hand of labor, be set into operation to transmute these raw materials into wealth, the finished products, in all their multiplied forms and in opulent abundance for all. The merest child can press a button that will set in operation a forest of machinery and produce wealth enough for a community.

Whatever may be said of the ignorant, barbarous past, there is no excuse for poverty today. And yet it is the scourge of the race. It is the Nemesis of capitalist civilization. Ten millions, one-eighth of our whole population, are in a state of chronic poverty. Three millions of these have been sunk to unresisting pauperism. The whole working class is in a sadly dependent state, and even the most favored wage-worker is left suspended by a single thread. He does not know what hour a machine may be invented to make his trade useless, displace him and throw him into the increasing army of the unemployed.

And how does labor live today? Here in Chicago you may walk along a certain boulevard, say 18th street, and you will find it lined with magnificent palaces. Beyond that you will find a larger district where the still complacent middle class abide. Beyond that is a very much larger territory where the working class exist; and still beyond that, to complete the circle, you see the red lights flickering in the distance.

Prostitution is a part, a necessary part, of capitalist society. The department store empties in the slums.

I have been here enough to know that when the daughter of a workingman is obliged to go up the street to look for employment, when she is fourteen or fifteen years of age, and ought to be in the care and keeping of a loving mother, and have all of the advantages that our civilization makes possible for all — when she is forced to go to a department store, to one of those capitalist emporiums, and there find a place, if she can, and work for a wage of $3 a week, and have to obey a code of cast-iron regulations, appear tidy and neatly dressed and be subjected to a thousand temptations daily, and then takes a misstep, the first, as she is more than apt to do, especially if she has no home in any decent sense of that term — the very instant this is added to her poverty, she is doomed — damned. All the doors of capitalist society are closed in her face. The coals of contumely are poured upon her head. There is for her no redemption, and she takes the next step, and the next, until at last she ends a disgraceful career in a brothel hell.

This may be your child. And if you are a workingman, and this should fall to the lot of the innocent blue-eyed child that you love more than you do your own life — I want you to realize that if such a horror be written in the book of fate, that you are responsible for it, if you use or misuse your power to perpetuate the capitalist system and working class slavery.

You can change this condition — not tomorrow, not next week, nor next year; but in the meantime the next thing to changing it is making up your mind that it shall be changed. That is what we Industrial Unionists have done. And so there has come to us a new state of mind, and in our hearts there is the joy of service and the serenity of triumph.

We are united and we cannot be disunited. We cannot be stampeded. We know that we are confronted by ten thousand difficulties. We know that all the powers of capitalism are to be arrayed against us. But were these obstacles multiplied by a million, it would simply have the effect of multiplying our determination by a million, to overcome them all. And so we are organizing and appealing to you.

The workingman today does not understand his industrial relation to his fellow-workers. He has never been correlated with others in the same industry. He has mechanically done his part. He has simply been a cog, with little reference to, or knowledge of, the rest of the cogs. Now, we teach him to hold up his head and look over the whole mechanism. If he is employed in a certain plant, as an Industrial Unionist, his eyes are opened. He takes a survey of the entire productive mechanism, and he understands his part in it, and his relation to every other worker in that industry. The very instant he does that he is buoyed by a fresh hope and thrilled with a new aspiration. He becomes a larger man. He begins to feel like a collective son of toil.

Then he and his fellows study to fit themselves to take control of this productive mechanism when it shall be transferred from the idle capitalist to the workers to whom it rightfully belongs.

In every mill and every factory, every mine and every quarry, every railroad and every shop, everywhere, the workers, enlightened, understanding their self-interest, are correlating themselves in the industrial and economic mechanism. They are developing their industrial consciousness, their economic and political power; and when the revolution comes, they will be prepared to take possession and assume control of every industry. With the education they will have received in the Industrial Workers they will be drilled and disciplined, trained and fitted for Industrial Mastery and Social Freedom.

Revolution

New York Worker April 27, 1907

This is the first and only International Labor Day. It belongs to the working class and is dedicated to the Revolution.

Today the slaves of all the world are taking a fresh breath in the long and weary march; pausing a moment to clear their lungs and shout for joy; celebrating in festal fellowship their coming Freedom.

All hail the Labor Day of May! The day of the proletarian protest; The day of stern resolve; The day of noble aspiration. Raise high this day the blood-red standard of the Revolution! The banner of the workingman; The flag, the only flag, of Freedom.

Slavery, even the most abject—dumb and despairing as it may seem—has yet its inspiration. Crushed it may be, but extinguished never. Chain the slave as you will, O Masters, brutalize him as you may, yet in his soul, though dead, he yearns for freedom still.

The great discovery the modern slaves have made is that they themselves their must achieve. This is the secret of their solidarity; the heart of their hope; the inspiration that nerves them all with sinews of steel.

They are still in bondage, but no longer cower;

No longer grovel in the dust,

But stand erect like men.

Conscious of their growing power the future holds up to them her outstretched hands.

As the slavery of the working class is international, so the movement for its emancipation.

The salutation of slave to slave this day is repeated in every human tongue as it goes ringing round the world.

The many millions are at last awakening. For countless ages they have suffered; drained to the dregs the bitter cup of misery and woe.

At last, at last the historic limitation has been reached, and soon a new sun will light the world.

Red is the life-tide of our common humanity and red our symbol of universal kinship.

Tyrants deny it; fear it; tremble with rage and terror when they behold it.

We reaffirm it and on this day pledge anew our fidelity — come life or death — to the blood-red Banner of the Revolution.

Socialist greetings this day to all our fellow-workers! To the god-like souls in Russia marching grimly, sublimely into the jaws of hell with the Song of the Revolution in their death-rattle; to the Orient, the Occident and all the Isles of the Sea!

VIVA LA REVOLUTION!

The most heroic word in all languages is REVOLUTION.

It thrills and vibrates; cheers and inspires. Tyrants and time-servers fear it, but the oppressed hail it with joy.

The throne trembles when this throbbing word is lisped, but to the hovel it is food for the famishing and hope for the victims of despair.

Let us glorify today the revolutions of the past and hail the Greater Revolution yet to come before Emancipation shall make all the days of the year May Days of peace and plenty for the sons and daughters of toil.

It was with Revolution as his theme that Mark Twain's soul drank deep from the fount of inspiration. His immortality will rest at last upon this royal tribute to the French Revolution:

"The ever memorable and blessed revolution, which swept a thousand years of villainy away in one swift tidal wave of blood—one: a settlement of that hoary debt in the proportion of half a drop of blood for each hogshead of it that had been pressed by slow tortures out of that people in the weary stretch of ten centuries of wrong and shame and misery the like of which was not to be mated but in hell. There were two Reigns of Terror, if we would but remember it and consider it: the one wrought murder in hot passion, the other in heartless cold blood; the one lasted mere months, the other lasted a thousand years; the one inflicted death on ten thousand persons, the other upon a hundred millions; but our shudders are all for the horrors of the minor Terror, so to speak; whereas, what is the horror of swift death by the axe compared with lifelong death from hunger, cold, insult, cruelty and heartbreak? What is swift death by lightning compared with death by slow fire at the stake? A city cemetery could contain the coffins filled by that brief Terror, which we have all been so diligently taught to shiver at and mourn over, but all France could hardly contain the coffins filled by that older and real Terror which none of us has been taught to see in its vastness or pity as it deserves."

Susan B. Anthony: A Reminiscence

Socialist Woman, January 1909.

Twice only did I personally meet Susan B. Anthony, although I knew her well. The first time was at Terre Haute, Indiana, my home, in 1880, and the last time shortly before her death at her home at Rochester, New York. I can never forget the first time I met her. She impressed me as being a wonderfully strong character, self-reliant, thoroughly in earnest, and utterly indifferent to criticism.

There was never a time in my life when I was opposed to the equal suffrage of the sexes. I could never understand why woman was denied any right or opportunity that man enjoyed. Quite early, therefore, I was attracted to the woman suffrage movement. I had of course read of Susan B. Anthony and from the ridicule and contempt with which she was treated I concluded that she must be a strong advocate of, and doing effective work for, the rights of her sex. It was then that I determined, with the aid of Mrs. Ida Husted Harper, the brilliant writer, who afterward became her biographer, to arrange a series of meetings for Miss Anthony at Terre Haute.

In due course of time I received a telegram from Miss Anthony from Lafayette announcing the time of her arrival at Terre Haute and asking me to meet her at the station. I recognized the distinguished lady or, to be more exact, the notorious woman, the instant she stepped from the train. She was accompanied by Lily Devereaux Blake and other woman suffrage agitators and I proceeded to escort them to the hotel where I had arranged for their reception.

I can still see the aversion so unfeelingly expressed for this magnificent woman. Even my friends were disgusted with me for piloting such an "undesirable citizen" into the community. It is hard to understand, after all these years, how bitter and implacable the people were, especially the women, toward the leaders of this movement.

As we walked along the street I was painfully aware that Miss Anthony was an object of derision and contempt, and in my heart I resented it and later I had often to defend my position, which, of course, I was ever ready to do.

The meetings of Miss Anthony and her co-workers were but poorly attended and all but barren of results. Such was the loathing of the community for a woman who dared to talk in public about "woman's rights" that people would not go to see her even to satisfy their curiosity. She was simply not to be tolerated and it would not have required any great amount of egging-on to have excited the people to drive her from the community.

To all of this Miss Anthony, to all appearance, was entirely oblivious. She could not have helped noticing it for there were those who thrust their insults upon her but she gave no sign and bore no resentment.

I can see her still as she walked along, neatly but carelessly attired, her bonnet somewhat awry, mere trifles which were scarcely noticed, if at all, in the presence of her splendid womanhood. She seemed absorbed completely in her mission. She could scarcely speak of anything else. The rights and wrongs of her sex seemed to completely possess her and to dominate all her thoughts and acts.

On the platform she spoke with characteristic earnestness and at times with such intensity as to awe her audience, if not compel conviction. She had an inexhaustible fund of information in regard to current affairs, and dates and data for all things. She spoke with great rapidity and forcefulness; her command of language was remarkable and her periods were all well-rounded and eloquently delivered. No thoughtful person could hear her without being convinced of her honesty and the purity of her motive. Her face fairly glowed with the spirit of her message and her soul was in her speech.

But the superb quality, the crowning virtue she possessed, was her moral heroism.

Susan B. Anthony had this quality in an eminent degree. She fearlessly faced the ignorant multitude or walked unafraid among those who scorned her. She had the dignity of perfect self-reliance without a shadow of conceit to mar it. She was a stern character, an uncompromising personality, but she had the heart of a woman and none more tender ever throbbed for the weak and the oppressed of earth.

No leader of any crusade was ever more fearless, loyal or uncompromising than Susan B. Anthony and not one ever wrought more unselfishly or under greater difficulties for the good of her kind and for the progress of the race.

I did not see Miss Anthony again until I shook hands with her at the close of my address in Rochester, but a short time before she passed to other realms. She was the same magnificent woman, but her locks had whitened and her kindly features bore the traces of age and infirmity.

Her life-work was done and her sun was setting!

How beautiful she seemed in the quiet serenity of her sunset!

Twenty-five years before she drank to its dregs the bitter cup of persecution, but now she stood upon the heights, a sad smile lighting her sweet face, amidst the acclaims of her neighbors and the plaudits of the world.

Susan B. Anthony freely consecrated herself to the service of humanity; she was a heroine in the highest sense and her name deserves a place among the highest on the scroll of the immortals.

Letter on Immigration

International Socialist Review, Vol. XI, No. 1. July 1910.

My Dear Brewer:

Have just read the majority report of the Committee on Immigration. It is utterly unsocialistic, reactionary and in truth outrageous, and I hope you will oppose with all your power. The plea that certain races are to be excluded because of tactical expediency would be entirely consistent in a bourgeois convention of self-seekers, but should have no place in a proletariat gathering under the auspices of an international movement that is calling on the oppressed and exploited workers of all the world to unite for their emancipation. . . .

Away with the "tactics" which require the exclusion of the oppressed and suffering slaves who seek these shores with the hope of bettering their wretched condition and are driven back under the cruel lash of expediency by those who call themselves

Socialists in the name of a movement whose proud boast it is that it stands uncompromisingly for the oppressed and down-trodden of all the earth. These poor slaves have just as good a right to enter here as even the authors of this report who now seek to exclude them. The only difference is that the latter had the advantage of a little education and had not been so cruelly ground and oppressed, but in point of principle there is no difference, the motive of all being precisely the same, and if the convention which meets in the name of Socialism should discriminate at all it should be in favor of the miserable races who have borne the heaviest burdens and are most nearly crushed to the earth.

Upon this vital proposition I would take my stand against the world and no specious argument of subtle and sophistical defenders of the civic federation unionism, who do not hesitate to sacrifice principle for numbers and jeopardize ultimate success for immediate gain, could move me to turn my back upon the oppressed, brutalized and despairing victims of the old world, who are lured to these shores by some faint glimmer of hope that here their crushing burdens may be lightened, and some star of promise rise in their darkened skies.

The alleged advantages that would come to the Socialist movement because of such heartless exclusion would all be swept away a thousand times by the sacrifice of a cardinal principle of the international socialist movement, for well might the good faith of such a movement be questioned by intelligent workers if it placed itself upon record as barring its doors against the very races most in need of relief, and extinguishing their hope, and leaving them in dark despair at the very time their ears were first attuned to the international call and their hearts were beginning to throb responsive to the solidarity of the oppressed of all lands and all climes beneath the skies.

In this attitude there is nothing of maudlin sentimentality, but simply a rigid adherence to the fundamental principles of the international proletarian movement. If Socialism, international, revolutionary Socialism, does not stand staunchly, unflinchingly, and uncompromisingly for the working class and for the exploited and oppressed masses of all lands, then it stands for none and its claim is a false pretense and its profession a delusion and a snare.

Let those desert us who will because we refuse to shut the international door in the faces of their own brethren; we will be none the weaker but all the stronger for their going, for they evidently have no clear conception of the international solidarity, are wholly lacking in the revolutionary spirit, and have no proper place in the Socialist movement while they entertain such aristocratic notions of their own assumed superiority.

Let us stand squarely on our revolutionary, working class principles and make our fight openly and uncompromisingly against all our enemies, adopting no cowardly tactics and holding out no false hopes, and our movement will then inspire the faith, arouse the spirit, and develop the fibre that will prevail against the world.

Yours without compromise,

Eugene V. Debs.

The Fight for Freedom

Campaign Speech, Pabst Park, Milwaukee, Wis., July 21, 1912.

Friends, Fellow-Socialists and Fellow-Workers: The existing order of things is breaking down. The great forces underlying society are steadily at work. The old order has had its day and all the signs point to an impending change. Society is at once being destroyed and re-created.

The struggle in which we are engaged today is a struggle of economic classes. The supremacy is now held by the capitalist class, who are combined in trusts and control the powers of government. The middle class is struggling desperately to hold its ground against the inroads of its trustified and triumphant competitors.

This war between the great capitalists who are organized in trusts and fortified by the powers of government and the smaller capitalists who constitute the middle class, is one of extermination. The fittest, that is to say the most powerful, will survive. This war gives rise to a variety of issues of which the tariff is the principal one, and these issues are defined in the platforms of the Republican and Democratic parties.

With this war between capitalists for supremacy in their own class and the issues arising from it, the working class have nothing to do, and if they are foolish enough to allow themselves to be drawn into these battles of their masters, as they have so often done in the past, they must continue to suffer the consequences of their folly.

Let us clearly recognize the forces that are undermining both of the old capitalist parties, creating a new issue, and driving the working class into a party of their own to do battle with their oppressors in the struggle for existence.

Parties but express in political terms the economic interests of those who compose them. This is the rule. The Republican party represents the capitalist class, the Democratic party the middle class and the Socialist party the working class.

There is no fundamental difference between the Republican and Democratic parties. Their principles are identical. They are both capitalist parties and both stand for the capitalist system, and such differences as there are between them involve no principle but are the outgrowth of the conflicting interests of large and small capitalists.

The Republican and Democratic parties are alike threatened with destruction. Their day of usefulness is past and they among them who see the handwriting on the wall and call themselves "Progressives" and "Insurgents," are struggling in vain to adjust these old parties to the new conditions.

Broadly speaking, there are but two economic classes and the ultimate struggle will narrow down to two political parties. To the extent that the workers unite in their own party, the Socialist party, the capitalists, large and small, are driven into one and the same party. This has happened already in a number of local instances, notably in the City of Milwaukee. Here there is no longer a Republican or Democratic party. These have merged in the same party and it is a capitalist party, by whatever name it may be known.

Temporarily this united capitalist party, composed of the two old ones, may stem the tide of Socialist advance, but nothing more clearly reveals the capitalist class character of the Republican and Democratic parties to their own undoing and the undoing of the capitalist system they represent.

The great capitalists are all conservatives, "standpatters"; they have a strangle-hold upon the situation with no intention of relaxing their grip. Taft and Roosevelt are their candidates. It may be objected that Roosevelt is a "Progressive." That is sheer buncombe. Roosevelt was president almost eight years and his record is known. When he was in office and had the power, he did none of the things, nor attempted to do any of the things he is now talking about so wildly. On the contrary, a more servile functionary to the trusts than Theodore Roosevelt never sat in the presidential chair.

Senator La Follette now makes substantially this same charge against Roosevelt, but by some strange oversight the senator did not discover that Roosevelt's presidential record was a trust record until after Roosevelt threw him down in the "Progressive" scramble for the Republican nomination.

When Senator La Follette supposed he had Roosevelt's backing, he pronounced him "the greatest man in the world," and it was only after he fell victim to Roosevelt's duplicity that he made the discovery that Roosevelt had always been the tool of the trusts and the enemy of the people.

There is one infallible test that fixes the status of a political party and its candidates. Who finances them?

With this test applied to Theodore Roosevelt we have no trouble in locating him. He is above all "a practical man." He was practical in allowing the steel trust to raid the Tennessee Coal and Iron Company; he was practical when he legalized the notorious "Alton Steal": he was practical when he had Harriman raise $240,000 for his campaign fund, and he is practical now in having the steel trust and the harvester trust, who made an anteroom of the White House when he was president, pour out their slush funds by millions to put him back in the White House and keep him there.

Taft and Roosevelt, and the Republican party of which they are the candidates, are all financed by the trusts, and is it necessary to add that the trusts also consist of practical men and that they do not finance a candidate or a party they do not control?

Is the man not foolish, to the verge of being feeble-minded, who imagines that great trust magnates, such as Perkins, McCormick and Munsey, are flooding the country with Roosevelt money because he is the champion of progressive principles and the friend of the common people?

The truth is that if the Bull Moose candidate dared to permit an itemized publication of his campaign contributions in his present mad and disgraceful pursuit of the presidency, as he has been so often challenged to do by Senator La Follette, it would paralyze him and scandalize the nation.

Roosevelt must stand upon the record he made when he was president and had the power, and not upon his empty promises as a ranting demagogue and a vote-seeking politician.

For the very reason that the trusts are pouring out their millions to literally buy his nomination and election and force him into the White House for a third term, and if possible for life, the people should rise in their might and repudiate him as they never have repudiated a recreant official who betrayed his trust.

So much for the Republican party, led by Lincoln half a century ago as the party of the people in the struggle for the overthrow of chattel slavery, and now being scuttled by Taft and Roosevelt in base servility to the plutocracy.

The Democratic party, like its Republican ally, is a capitalist party, the only difference being that it represents the minor divisions of the capitalist class. It is true that there are some plutocrats and trust magnates in the Democratic party, but as a rule it is composed of the smaller capitalists who have been worsted by the larger ones and are now demanding that the trusts be destroyed and, in effect, that the laws of industrial evolution be suspended.

The Democratic party, like the Republican party, is financed by the capitalist class. Belmont, Ryan, Roger Sullivan, Taggart and Hinky Dink are liberal contributors to its fund. The Tammany organization in New York, notorious for its corruption and for its subserviency to the powers that rule in capitalist society, is one of the controlling factors in the Democratic party.

Woodrow Wilson is the candidate of the Democratic party for president. He was seized upon as a "progressive"; as a man who would appeal to the common people, but he never could have been nominated without the votes controlled by Tammany and the "predatory interests" so fiercely denounced in the convention by William Jennings Bryan.

It is true that Woodrow Wilson was not the first choice of Belmont, Ryan, Murphy and the Tammany corruptionists, but he was nevertheless satisfactory to them or they would not have agreed to his nomination, and since the convention it is quite apparent that Wilson has a working agreement and a perfect understanding with the predatory interests which Bryan sought to scourge from the convention.

In his speech before the delegates denouncing Ryan, Belmont and Murphy, Bryan solemnly declared that no candidate receiving their votes and the votes of Murphy's "ninety wax figures" could have his support. Woodrow Wilson received these votes and without these and other votes controlled by "the interests" he could not have been nominated, and if Bryan now supports him he simply stultifies himself before the American people.

Mr. Wilson is no more the candidate of the working class than is Mr. Taft or Mr. Roosevelt. Neither one of them has ever been identified with the working class, has ever associated with the working class, except when their votes were wanted, or would dare to avow himself the candidate of the working class.

When the recent strikes occurred at Perth Amboy and other industrial centers in New Jersey, Governor Woodrow Wilson ordered the militia out to shoot down the strikers just as Governor Theodore Roosevelt ordered out the soldiers to murder the strikers at Croton Dam, N.Y., for demanding the enforcement of the state laws against the contractors.

Both the Republican and Democratic parties reek with corruption in their servility to the capitalist class, and both are torn with strife in their mad scramble for the spoils of office.

The Democratic party has had little excuse for existence since the Civil War, and its utter impotency to deal with present conditions was made glaringly manifest during its brief lease of power under the Cleveland administration. Should this party succeed to national power once more, seething as it is with conflicting elements which are held together by the prospect of official spoils, its career as a national party would be brought to an early close by self-destruction.

The Republican convention at Chicago and the Democratic convention at Baltimore were composed of professional politicians, office-holders, office-seekers, capitalists, retainers, and swarms of parasites and mercenaries of all descriptions.

There were no workingmen in either convention. They were not fit to be there. All they are fit for is to march in the mud, yell themselves hoarse, and ratify the choice of their masters on election day.

The working class was not represented in the Republican convention at Chicago or the Democratic convention at Baltimore. Those were the political conventions of the capitalist class and the few flattering platform phrases in reference to labor were incorporated for the sole purpose of catching the votes of the working class.

Let the American workers remember that they are not fit to sit as delegates in a Republican or Democratic national convention; that they are not fit to write a Republican or Democratic national platform; that all they are fit for is to elect the candidates of their masters to office so that when they go out on strike against starvation they may be shot dead in their tracks as the reward of their servility to their masters and their treason to themselves.

The vital issue before the country and the world is not touched, nor even mentioned in the Republican or Democratic platforms. Wage-slavery under capitalism, the legalized robbery of the workers of what is produced by their labor, is the fundamental crime against modern humanity, but there is no room for the mention of this vital fact, this living issue in the platforms of the Republican and Democratic parties. They continue to babble about the tariff and other inconsequential matters to obscure the real issue and wheedle the workers into voting them into power once more.

These parties have been in power all these years, why have they not settled the tariff and the currency and such other matters as make up their platform pledges?

While the Republican convention was in session at Chicago and while the Democratic convention was in session at Baltimore, the Republican and Democratic congress was also in session at Washington. These parties already have the power to make good their promises, then why do they not exercise that power to redeem their pledges and afford relief to the people?

In other words, why do not the Republican and Democratic parties perform at Washington instead of promising at Chicago and Baltimore? How many more years of power do they require to demonstrate that they are the parties of the capitalist class and that they never intend to legislate in the interest of the working class, or provide relief for the suffering people.

The Republican and Democratic platforms are filled with empty platitudes and meaningless phrases, but they are discreetly silent about the millions of unemployed, about the starvation wages of factory slaves, about the women and children who are crushed, debased and slowly tortured to death by the Moloch of capitalism, about the white slave traffic, about the bitter poverty of the masses and their hopeless future, and about every other vital question which is worthy of an instant's consideration by any intelligent human being.

In contrast with these impotent, corrupt and senile capitalist parties, without principles and without ideals, stands the virile young working class party, the international Socialist party of the world. The convention which nominated its candidates and wrote its platform at Indianapolis was a working class convention.

The Socialist party is the only party which honestly represents the working class in this campaign and the only party that has a moral right to appeal to the allegiance and support of the workers and producers of the nation.

I am not asking you to give your votes to this party but only that you read its platform, study its program, and satisfy yourselves as to what its principles are, what it stands for, and what it expects to accomplish.

The Socialist party being the political expression of the rising working class stands for the absolute overthrow of the existing capitalist system and for the reorganization of society into an industrial and social democracy

This will mean an end to the private ownership of the means of life; it will mean an end to wage slavery; it will mean an end to the army of the unemployed; it will mean an end to the poverty of the masses, the prostitution of womanhood, and the murder of childhood.

It will mean the beginning of a new era of civilization; the dawn of a happier day for the children of men. It will mean that this earth is for those who inhabit it and wealth for those who produce it. It will mean society organized upon a co-operative basis, collectively owning the sources of wealth and the means of production, and producing wealth to satisfy human wants and not to gorge a privileged few. It will mean that there shall be work for the workers and that all shall be workers, and it will also mean that there shall be leisure for the workers and that all shall enjoy it. It will mean that women shall be the comrades and equals of men, sharing with them on equal terms the opportunities as well as the responsibilities, the benefits as well as the burdens of civilized life.

The Socialist party, the first and only international party, is rising grandly to power all around the world. In every land beneath the sun it is the party of the dispossessed, the impoverished and the heavy-laden.

It is the twentieth century party of human emancipation.

It stands for a world-wide democracy, for the freedom of every man, woman and child, and for the civilization of all mankind.

The Socialist party buys no votes. It scorns to traffic in ignorance. It realizes that education, knowledge and the powers these confer are the only means of achieving a decided and permanent victory for the people.

The campaign of the Socialist party is a clean campaign; it is essentially educational; an appeal to intelligence, to manliness, to womanliness, and to all things of good report.

The workers are opening their eyes at last. They are beginning to see the light. They are taking heart of hope because they are becoming conscious of their power.

They are rallying to the standard of the Socialist party because they know that this is their party and that here they are master, and here they sit at their own political hearthstone and fireside.

No longer can the workers be pitted against each other in capitalist parties by designing politicians to their mutual undoing. They have made the discovery that they have brains as well as hands, that they can think as well as work, and that they do not need politicians to advise them how to vote, nor masters to rob them of the fruits of their labor.

Slowly but surely there is being established the economic and political unity and solidarity of the workers of the world. The Socialist party is the political expression of that unity and solidarity.

I appeal to the workers assembled here today in the name of the Socialist party. I appeal to you as one of you to unite and make common cause in this great struggle.

To the extent that you have made progress, to the extent that you have developed power, and to the extent that you have achieved victory, to that extent you are indebted to your own class-conscious efforts and your own industrial and political organization. To the extent that you lack power, to the extent that you are defeated and kept in bondage, to that extent you lack in economic and political solidarity.

Rightly organized and soundly disciplined on both the economic and political fields, the working class can prevail against the world.

The economic organization and the political party of the working class must both be revolutionary and they must work together hand in hand. Industrial unionism means industrial solidarity, but craft unionism means division and disaster. The printing trades pitted against each other in Chicago in their struggle with the newspaper trust furnish a fatal illustration of the weakness and treachery of craft division in the present industrial conflict.

The workers of Milwaukee have to an exceptional extent overcome the obstacles to unity and have worked together with signal success on both the economic and political fields. I appeal to them in the name of the future to get closer and closer together in the bonds of economic and political solidarity. If they do this their complete arid final victory is assured.

The Socialist party of Milwaukee has marched steadily to the front since it first began its career. Its latest defeat was its greatest victory. It forced the Republicans and Democrats to unmask and to fly into each other's arms. There is no Republican or Democratic party in Milwaukee. They are dead, and in the coming election their remains, masquerading as a party of the people, will be buried by the Socialist party.

The Socialists of Milwaukee will always have the distinction of having elected the first representative of the working class to the congress of the United States. Victor L. Berger has made good at Washington. For the first time since he is a member the voice of labor has been distinctly heard on the floors of congress, and in every emergency when the working class needed a champion at the seat of power, they found him ready and eager to espouse their cause and defend their interests.

It was to defeat Berger's re-election that the Republicans and Democrats in Milwaukee combined, just as they did to defeat Emil Seidel for mayor and drive the Socialist administration from power.

But Berger is making a record at Washington and the Socialist administration made a record in Milwaukee that will stand the test of time, and if the workers now rally their forces in support of Berger, he will be triumphantly re-elected against the combined opposition of the old parties, and in the next municipal election the City of Milwaukee will be permanently restored to a Socialist administration.

Comrades, you are face to face with the greatest struggle you have ever had since the Socialist party was organized. You are now to be tested in every fiber as to your fitness to hold the ground you have gained and to press on to greater victories. May you be permeated to the core with the spirit of the Socialist movement and enter the fray resolved that victory shall be inscribed upon your banners.

I must not fail in the presence of all these workers to speak of Joseph Ettor and Arturo Giovannitti, the leaders of the Lawrence strike, who are in prison and soon to be tried upon the charge of murder, of which they are as innocent as if they had never been born.

This infamous charge has been trumped up against them by the defeated mill owners for no other reason than that they stood up bravely and fought successfully against great odds, the battles of the wage-slaves of the mills. Unless the workers unite in support of these two leaders they may be sent to the electric chair. Should we suffer these brave comrades to fall victims to such a monstrous crime, it would be a foul and indelible blot upon the whole labor movement. Let us arouse the workers of the nation in their behalf and prove to them when their trial takes place that we are as true to them as they were to the wage-slaves in the industrial battle at Lawrence.

Comrades, this is our year! Let us rise to our full stature, summon our united powers, and strike a blow for freedom that will be felt around the world!

The Prospect for Peace

American Socialist, February 19, 1916

There is no doubt that the belligerent nations of Europe are all heartily sick of war and that they would all welcome peace even if they could not dictate all its terms.

But it should not be overlooked that this frightful upheaval is but a symptom of the international readjustment which the underlying economic forces are bringing about, as well as the fundamental changes which are being wrought in our industrial and political institutions. Still, every war must end and so must this. The destruction of both life and property has been so appalling during the eighteen months that the war has been waged that we may well conclude that the fury of the conflict is largely spent and that, with bankruptcy and ruin such as the world never beheld staring them in the face, the lords of capitalist misrule are about ready to sue for peace.

From the point of view of the working class, the chief sufferers in this as in every war, the most promising indication of peace is the international conference recently held in Zimmerwald, Switzerland, attended by representatives of all European neutral nations and some of the belligerent powers. This conference, consisting wholly of representatives of the working class issued a ringing manifesto in favor of the international re-organization on a permanent and uncompromising anti-war basis and of putting forth all possible efforts to end the bloody conflict which for a year and a half has shocked Christendom and outraged the civilization of the world.

The manifesto above referred to has been received with enthusiasm by the workers of all of the belligerent nations and the sentiment in favor of its acceptance and of the program of procedure it lays down is spreading rapidly in labor circles in the nations at war as well as in those at peace.

It would no doubt do much to clear the situation and expedite peace overtures if a decisive battle were fought and the indications are that such a battle, or series of battles, will be fought between now and spring. But the opportune moment for pressing peace negotiations can be determined only by the logic of events and when this comes the people of the United States should be ready to help in every way in their power to terminate this unholy massacre and bring peace to the world.

As to the terms upon which peace is to be restored these will no doubt be determined mainly by the status of the several belligerent powers when the war is ended. A program of disarmament looking to the prevention of another such catastrophe would seem to be suggested by the present heart-breaking situation but as experience has demonstrated that capitalist nations have no honor and that the most solemn treaty is but a "scrap of paper" in their mad rivalry for conquest and plunder, such a program, even if adopted, might prove abortive and barren of results.

The matter of the conquered provinces will no doubt figure largely in the peace negotiations and the only way to settle that in accordance with the higher principles of civilized nations is to allow the people of each province in dispute to decide for themselves by popular vote what nation they desire to be annexed to, or to remain, if they prefer, independent sovereignties.

Permanent peace, however; peace based upon social justice, will never prevail until national industrial despotism has been supplanted by international industrial democracy. The end of profit and plunder among nations will also mean the end of war and the dawning of the era of "Peace on Earth and Good Will among Men."

The Canton, Ohio Speech

Anti-War Speech Delivered June 16, 1918

Comrades, friends and fellow-workers, for this very cordial greeting, this very hearty reception, I thank you all with the fullest appreciation of your interest in and your devotion to the cause for which I am to speak to you this afternoon.

To speak for labor; to plead the cause of the men and women and children who toil; to serve the working class, has always been to me a high privilege; a duty of love.

I have just returned from a visit over yonder, where three of our most loyal comrades are paying the penalty for their devotion to the cause of the working class. They have come to realize, as many of us have, that it is extremely dangerous to exercise the constitutional right of free speech in a country fighting to make democracy safe in the world.

I realize that, in speaking to you this afternoon, there are certain limitations placed upon the right of free speech. I must be exceedingly careful, prudent, as to what I say, and even more careful and prudent as to how I say it. I may not be able to say all I think; but I am not going to say anything that I do not think. I would rather a thousand times be a free soul in jail than to be a sycophant and coward in the streets. They may put those boys in jail—and some of the rest of us in jail—but they can not put the Socialist movement in jail. Those prison bars separate their bodies from ours, but their souls are here this afternoon. They are simply paying the penalty that all men have paid in all the ages of history for standing erect, and for seeking to pave the way to better conditions for mankind.

If it had not been for the men and women who, in the past, have had the moral courage to go to jail, we would still be in the jungles.

This assemblage is exceedingly good to look upon. I wish it were possible for me to give you what you are giving me this afternoon. What I say here amounts to but little; what I see here is exceedingly important. You workers in Ohio, enlisted in the greatest cause ever organized in the interest of your class, are making history today in the face of threatening opposition of all kinds—history that is going to be read with profound interest by coming generations.

There is but one thing you have to be concerned about, and that is that you keep foursquare with the principles of the international Socialist movement. It is only when you begin to compromise that trouble begins. So far as I am concerned, it does not matter what others may say, or think, or do, as long as I am sure that I am right with myself and the cause. There are so many who seek refuge in the popular side of a great question. As a Socialist, I have long since learned how to stand alone. For the last month I have been traveling over the Hoosier State; and, let me say to you, that, in all my connection with the Socialist movement, I have never seen such meetings, such enthusiasm, such unity of purpose; never have I seen such a promising outlook as there is today, notwithstanding the statement published repeatedly that our leaders have deserted us. Well, for myself, I never had much faith in leaders. I am willing to be charged with almost anything, rather than to be charged with being a leader. I am suspicious of leaders, and especially of the intellectual variety. Give me the rank and file every day in the week. If you go to the city of Washington, and you examine the pages of the Congressional Directory, you will find that almost all of those corporation lawyers and cowardly politicians, members of Congress, and misrepresentatives of the masses— you will find that almost all of them claim, in glowing terms, that they have risen from the ranks to places of eminence and distinction. I am very glad I cannot make that claim for myself. I would be ashamed to admit that I had risen from the ranks. When I rise it will be with the ranks, and not from the ranks.

When I came away from Indiana, the comrades said: "When you cross the line and get over into the Buckeye State, tell the comrades there that we are on duty and doing duty. Give them for us, a hearty greeting, and tell them that we are going to make a record this fall that will be read around the world."

The Socialists of Ohio, it appears, are very much alive this year. The party has been killed recently, which, no doubt, accounts for its extraordinary activity. There is nothing that helps the Socialist Party so much as receiving an occasional deathblow. The oftener it is killed the more active, the more energetic, the more powerful it becomes.

They who have been reading the capitalist newspapers realize what a capacity they have for lying. We have been reading them lately. They know all about the Socialist Party— the Socialist movement—except what is true. Only the other day they took an article that I had written—and most of you have read it—most of you members of the party, at least—and they made it appear that I had undergone a marvelous transformation. I had suddenly become changed—had in fact come to my senses; I had ceased to be a wicked Socialist, and had become a respectable Socialist, a patriotic Socialist—as if I had ever been anything else.

What was the purpose of this deliberate misrepresentation? It is so self-evident that it suggests itself. The purpose was to sow the seeds of dissension in our ranks; to have it appear that we were divided among ourselves; that we were pitted against each other, to our mutual undoing. But Socialists were not born yesterday. They know how to read capitalist newspapers; and to believe exactly the opposite of what they read.

Why should a Socialist be discouraged on the eve of the greatest triumph in all the history of the Socialist movement? It is true that these are anxious, trying days for us all—testing days for the women and men who are upholding the banner of labor in the struggle of the working class of all the world against the exploiters of all the world; a time in which the weak and cowardly will falter and fail and desert. They lack the fiber to endure the revolutionary test; they fall away; they disappear as if they had never been. On the other hand, they who are animated by the unconquerable spirit of the social revolution; they who have the moral courage to stand erect and assert their convictions; stand by them; fight for them; go to jail or to hell for them, if need be —they are writing their names, in this crucial hour—they are writing their names in faceless letters in the history of mankind.

Those boys over yonder—those comrades of ours—and how I love them! Aye, they are my younger brothers; their very names throb in my heart, thrill in my veins, and surge in my soul. I am proud of them; they are there for us; and we are here for them. Their lips, though temporarily mute, are more eloquent than ever before; and their voice, though silent, is heard around the world.

Are we opposed to Prussian militarism? Why, we have been fighting it since the day the Socialist movement was born; and we are going to continue to fight it, day and night, until it is wiped from the face of the earth. Between us there is no truce— no compromise.

But, before I proceed along this line, let me recall a little history, in which I think we are all interested.

In 1869 that grand old warrior of the social revolution, the elder Liebknecht, was arrested and sentenced to prison for three months, because of his war, as a Socialist, on the Kaiser and on the Junkers that rule Germany. In the meantime the Franco-Prussian war broke out. Liebknecht and Bebel were the Socialist members in the Reichstag. They were the only two who had the courage to protest against taking Alsace-Lorraine from France and annexing it to Germany. And for this they were sentenced two years to a prison fortress charged with high treason; because, even in that early day, almost fifty years ago, these leaders, these forerunners of the international Socialist movement were fighting the Kaiser and fighting the Junkers of Germany. They have continued to fight them from that day to this. Multiplied thousands of Socialists have languished in the jails of Germany because of their heroic warfare upon the despotic ruling class of that country.

Let us come down the line a little farther. You remember that, at the close of Theodore Roosevelt's second term as President, he went over to Africa to make war on some of his ancestors. You remember that, at the close of his expedition, he visited the capitals of Europe; and that he was wined and dined, dignified and glorified by all the Kaisers and Czars and Emperors of the Old World. He visited Potsdam while the Kaiser was there; and, according to the accounts published in the American newspapers, he and the Kaiser were soon on the most familiar terms. They were hilariously intimate with each other, and slapped each other on the back. After Roosevelt had reviewed the Kaiser's troops, according to the same accounts, he became enthusiastic over the Kaiser's legions and said: "If I had that kind of an army, I could conquer the world." He knew the Kaiser then just as well as he knows him now. He knew that he was the Kaiser, the Beast of Berlin. And yet, he permitted himself to be entertained by that Beast of Berlin; had his feet under the mahogany of the Beast of Berlin; was cheek by jowl with the Beast of Berlin. And, while Roosevelt was being entertained royally by the German Kaiser, that same Kaiser was putting the leaders of the Socialist Party in jail for fighting the Kaiser and the Junkers of Germany. Roosevelt was the guest of honor in the white house of the Kaiser, while the Socialists were in the jails of the Kaiser for fighting the Kaiser. Who then was fighting for democracy? Roosevelt? Roosevelt, who was honored by the Kaiser, or the Socialists who were in jail by order of the Kaiser?

"Birds of a feather flock together."

When the newspapers reported that Kaiser Wilhelm and ex-President Theodore recognized each other at sight, were perfectly intimate with each other at the first touch, they made the admission that is fatal to the claim of Theodore Roosevelt, that he is the friend of the common people and the champion of democracy; they admitted that they were kith and kin; that they were very much alike; that their ideas and ideals were about the same. If Theodore Roosevelt is the great champion of democracy — the arch foe of autocracy, what business had he as the guest of honor of the Prussian Kaiser? And when he met the Kaiser, and did honor to the Kaiser, under the terms imputed to him, wasn't it pretty strong proof that he himself was a Kaiser at heart? Now, after being the guest of Emperor Wilhelm, the Beast of Berlin, he comes back to this country, and wants you to send ten million men over there to kill the Kaiser; to murder his former friend and pal. Rather queer, isn't it? And yet, he is the patriot, and we are the traitors. I challenge you to find a Socialist anywhere on the face of the earth who was ever the guest of the Beast of Berlin, except as an inmate of his prison — the elder Liebknecht and the younger Liebknecht, the heroic son of his immortal sire.

A little more history along the same line. In 1902 Prince Henry paid a visit to this country. Do you remember him? I do, exceedingly well. Prince Henry is the brother of Emperor Wilhelm. Prince Henry is another Beast of Berlin, an autocrat, an aristocrat, a Junker of Junkers — very much despised by our American patriots. He came over here in 1902 as the representative of Kaiser Wilhelm; he was received by Congress and by several state legislatures—among others, by the state legislature of Massachusetts, then in session. He was invited there by the capitalist captains of that so-called commonwealth. And when Prince Henry arrived, there was one member of that body who kept his self-respect, put on his hat, and as Henry, the Prince, walked in, that member of the body walked out. And that was James F. Carey, the Socialist member of that body. All the rest—all the rest of the representatives in the Massachusetts legislature—all, all of them—joined in doing honor, in the most servile spirit, to the high representative of the autocracy of Europe. And the only man who left that body, was a Socialist. And yet, and yet they have the hardihood to claim that they are fighting autocracy and that we are in the service of the German government.

A little more history along the same line. I have a distinct recollection of it. It occurred fifteen years ago when Prince Henry came here. All of our plutocracy, all of the wealthy representatives living along Fifth Avenue—all, all of them— threw their palace doors wide open and received Prince Henry with open arms. But they were not satisfied with this; they got down and groveled in the dust at his feet. Our plutocracy— women and men alike—vied with each other to lick the boots of Prince Henry, the brother and representative of the "Beast of Berlin." And still our plutocracy, our Junkers, would have us believe that all the Junkers are confined to Germany. It is precisely because we refuse to believe this that they brand us as disloyalists. They want our eyes focused on the Junkers in Berlin so that we will not see those within our own borders.

I hate, I loathe, I despise Junkers and junkerdom. I have no earthly use for the Junkers of Germany, and not one particle more use for the Junkers in the United States.

They tell us that we live in a great free republic; that our institutions are democratic; that we are a free and self-governing people. This is too much, even for a joke. But it is not a subject for levity; it is an exceedingly serious matter.

To whom do the Wall Street Junkers in our country marry their daughters? After they have wrung their countless millions from your sweat, your agony and your life's blood, in a time of war as in a time of peace, they invest these untold millions in the purchase of titles of broken-down aristocrats, such as princes, dukes, counts and other parasites and no-accounts. Would they be satisfied to wed their daughters to honest workingmen? To real democrats? Oh, no! They scour the markets of Europe for vampires who are titled and nothing else. And they swap their millions for the titles, so that matrimony with them becomes literally a matter of money.

These are the gentry who are today wrapped up in the American flag, who shout their claim from the housetops that they are the only patriots, and who have their magnifying glasses in hand, scanning the country for evidence of disloyalty, eager to apply the brand of treason to the men who dare to even whisper their opposition to Junker rule in the United States. No wonder Sam Johnson declared that "patriotism is the last refuge of the scoundrel." He must have had this Wall Street gentry in mind, or at least their prototypes, for in every age it has been the tyrant, the oppressor and the exploiter who has wrapped himself in the cloak of patriotism, or religion, or both to deceive and overawe the people.

They would have you believe that the Socialist Party consists in the main of disloyalists and traitors. It is true in a sense not at all to their discredit. We frankly admit that we are disloyalists and traitors to the real traitors of this nation; to the gang that on the Pacific coast are trying to hang Tom Mooney and Warren Billings in spite of their well-known innocence and the protest of practically the whole civilized world.

I know Tom Mooney intimately—as if he were my own brother. He is an absolutely honest man. He had no more to do with the crime with which he was charged and for which he was convicted than I had. And if he ought to go to the gallows, so ought I. If he is guilty every man who belongs to a labor organization or to the Socialist Party is likewise guilty.

What is Tom Mooney guilty of? I will tell you. I am familiar with his record. For years he has been fighting bravely and without compromise the battles of the working class out on the Pacific coast. He refused to be bribed and he could not be browbeaten. In spite of all attempts to intimidate him he continued loyally in the service of the organized workers, and for this he became a marked man. The henchmen of the powerful and corrupt corporations, concluding finally that he could not be bought or bribed or bullied, decided he must therefore be murdered. That is why Tom Mooney is today a life prisoner, and why he would have been hanged as a felon long ago but for the world-wide protest of the working class.

Let us review another bit of history. You remember Francis J. Heney, special investigator of the state of California, who was shot down in cold blood in the courtroom in San Francisco. You remember that dastardly crime, do you not? The United Railways, consisting of a lot of plutocrats and highbinders represented by the Chamber of Commerce, absolutely control the city of San Francisco. The city was and is their private reservation. Their will is the supreme law. Take your stand against them and question their authority, and you are doomed. They do not hesitate a moment to plot murder or any other crime to perpetuate their corrupt and enslaving regime. Tom Mooney was the chief representative of the working class they could not control. They own the railways; they control the great industries; they are the industrial masters and the political rulers of the people. From their decision there is no appeal. They are the autocrats of the Pacific coast—as cruel and infamous as any that ever ruled in Germany or any other country in the old world. When their rule became so corrupt that at last a grand jury indicted them and they were placed on trial, and Francis J. Heney was selected to assist in their prosecution, this gang, represented by the Chamber of Commerce; this gang of plutocrats, autocrats and highbinders, hired an assassin to shoot Heney down in the courtroom. Heney, however, happened to live through it. But that was not their fault. The same identical gang that hired the murderer to kill Heney also hired false witnesses to swear away the fife of Tom Mooney and, foiled in that, they have kept him in a foul prisonhole ever since.

Every solitary one of these aristocratic conspirators and would-be murderers claims to be an arch-patriot; every one of them insists that the war is being waged to make the world safe for democracy. What humbug! What rot! What false pretense! These autocrats, these tyrants, these red-handed robbers and murderers, the "patriots," while the men who have the courage to stand face to face with them, speak the truth, and fight for their exploited victims—they are the disloyalists and traitors. If this be true, I want to take my place side by side with the traitors in this fight.

The other day they sentenced Kate Richards O'Hare to the penitentiary for five years. Think of sentencing a woman to the penitentiary simply for talking. The United States, under plutocratic rule, is the only country that would send a woman to prison for five years for exercising the right of free speech. If this be treason, let them make the most of it.

Let me review a bit of history in connection with this case. I have known Kate Richards O'Hare intimately for twenty years. I am familiar with her public record. Personally I know her as if she were my own sister. All who know Mrs. O'Hare know her to be a woman of unquestioned integrity." And they also know that she is a woman of unimpeachable loyalty to the Socialist movement. When she went out into North Dakota to make her speech, followed by plain-clothes men in the service of the government intent upon effecting her arrest and securing her prosecution and conviction—when she went out there, it was with the full knowledge on her part that sooner or later these detectives would accomplish their purpose. She made her speech, and that speech was deliberately misrepresented for the purpose of securing her conviction. The only testimony against her was that of a hired witness. And when the farmers, the men and women who were in the audience she addressed—when they went to Bismarck where the trial was held to testify in her favor, to swear that she had not used the language she was charged with having used, the judge refused to allow them to go upon the stand. This would seem incredible to me if I had not had some experience of my own with federal courts.

Who appoints our federal judges? The people? In all the history of the country, the working class have never named a federal judge. There are 121 of these judges and every solitary one holds his position, his tenure, through the influence and power of corporate capital. The corporations and trusts dictate their appointment. And when they go to the bench, they go, not to serve, the people, but to serve the interests that place them and keep them where they are.

Why, the other day, by a vote of five to four—a kind of craps game—come seven, come eleven —they declared the child labor law unconstitutional—a law secured after twenty years of education and agitation on the part of all kinds of people. And yet, by a majority of one, the Supreme Court a body of corporation lawyers, with just one exception, wiped that law from the statute books, and this in our so-called democracy, so that we may continue to grind the flesh and blood and bones of puny little children into profits for the Junkers of Wall Street. And this in a country that boasts of fighting to make the world safe for democracy! The history of this country is being written in the blood of the childhood the industrial lords have murdered.

These are not palatable truths to them. They do not like to hear them; and what is more they do not want you to hear them. And that is why they brand us as undesirable citizens, and as disloyalists and traitors. If we were actual traitors— traitors to the people and to their welfare and progress, we would be regarded as eminently respectable citizens of the republic; we would hold high office, have princely incomes, and ride in limousines; and we would be pointed out as the elect who have succeeded in life in honorable pursuit, and worthy of emulation by the youth of the land. It is precisely because we are disloyal to the traitors that we are loyal to the people of this nation.

Scott Nearing! You have heard of Scott Nearing. He is the greatest teacher in the United States. He was in the University of Pennsylvania until the Board of Trustees, consisting of great capitalists, captains of industry, found that he was teaching sound economics to the students in his classes. This sealed his fate in that institution. They sneeringly charged—just as the same usurers, money-changers, pharisees, hypocrites charged the Judean Carpenter some twenty centuries ago—that he was a false teacher and that he was stirring up the people.

The Man of Galilee, the Carpenter, the workingman who became the revolutionary agitator of his day soon found himself to be an undesirable citizen in the eyes of the ruling knaves and they had him crucified. And now their lineal descendants say of Scott Nearing, "He is preaching false economics. We cannot crucify him as we did his elder brother but we can deprive him of employment and so cut off his income and starve him to death or into submission. We will not only discharge him but place his name upon the blacklist and make it impossible for him to earn a living. He is a dangerous man for he is teaching the truth and opening the eyes of the people." And the truth, oh, the truth has always been unpalatable and intolerable to the class who live out of the sweat and misery of the working class.

Max Eastman has been indicted and his paper suppressed, just as the papers with which I have been connected have all been suppressed. What a wonderful compliment they pay us! They are afraid that we may mislead and contaminate you. You are their wards; they are your guardians and they know what is best for you to read and hear and know. They are bound to see to it that our vicious doctrines do not reach your ears. And so in our great democracy, under our free institutions, they flatter our press by suppression; and they ignorantly imagine that they have silenced revolutionary propaganda in the United States. What an awful mistake they make for our benefit! As a matter of justice to them we should respond with resolutions of thanks and gratitude. Thousands of people who had never before heard of our papers are now inquiring for and insisting upon seeing them. They have succeeded only in arousing curiosity in our literature and propaganda. And woe to him who reads Socialist literature from curiosity! He is surely a goner. I have known of a thousand experiments but never one that failed.

John M. Work! You know John, now on the editorial staff of the *Milwaukee Leader*! When I first knew him he was a lawyer out in Iowa. The capitalists out there became alarmed because of the rapid growth of the Socialist movement. So they said: "We have to find some able fellow to fight this menace." They concluded that John Work was the man for the job and they said to him: "John, you are a bright young lawyer; you have a brilliant future before you. We want to engage you to find out all you can about socialism and then proceed to counteract its baneful effects and check its further growth."

John at once provided himself with Socialist literature and began his study of the red menace, with the result that after he had read and digested a few volumes he was a full-fledged Socialist and has been fighting for socialism ever since.

How stupid and shortsighted the ruling class really is! Cupidity is stone blind. It has no vision. The greedy, profit-seeking exploiter cannot see beyond the end of his nose. He can see a chance for an "opening"; he is cunning enough to know what graft is and where it is, and how it can be secured, but vision he has none—not the slightest. He knows nothing of the great throbbing world that spreads out in all directions. He has no capacity for literature; no appreciation of art; no soul for beauty. That is the penalty the parasites pay for the violation of the laws of life. The Rockefellers are blind. Every move they make in their game of greed but hastens their own doom. Every blow they strike at the Socialist movement reacts upon themselves. Every time they strike at us they hit themselves. It never fails. Every time they strangle a Socialist paper they add a thousand voices proclaiming the truth of the principles of socialism and the ideals of the Socialist movement. They help us in spite of themselves.

Socialism is a growing idea; an expanding philosophy. It is spreading over the entire face of the earth: It is as vain to resist it as it would be to arrest the sunrise on the morrow. It is coming, coming, coming all along the line. Can you not see it? If not, I advise you to consult an oculist. There is certainly something the matter with your vision. It is the mightiest movement in the history of mankind. What a privilege to serve it! I have regretted a thousand times that I can do so little for the movement that has done so much for me. The little that I am, the little that I am hoping to be, I owe to the Socialist movement. It has given me my ideas and ideals; my principles and convictions, and I would not exchange one of them for all of Rockefeller's bloodstained dollars. It has taught me how to serve—a lesson to me of priceless value. It has taught me the ecstasy in the handclasp of a comrade. It has enabled me to hold high communion with you, and made it possible for me to take my place side by side with you in the great struggle for the better day; to multiply myself over and over again, to thrill with a fresh-born manhood; to feel life truly worthwhile; to open new avenues of vision; to spread out glorious vistas; to know that I am kin to all that throbs; to be class-conscious, and to realize that, regardless of nationality, race, creed, color or sex, every man, every woman who toils, who renders useful service, every member of the working class without an exception, is my comrade, my brother and sister—and that to serve them and their cause is the highest duty of my life.

And in their service I can feel myself expand; I can rise to the stature of a man and claim the right to a place on earth—a place where I can stand and strive to speed the day of industrial freedom and social justice.

Yes, my comrades, my heart is attuned to yours. Aye, all our hearts now throb as one great heart responsive to the battle cry of the social revolution. Here, in this alert and inspiring assemblage our hearts are with the Bolsheviki of Russia. Those heroic men and women, those unconquerable comrades have by their incomparable valor and sacrifice added fresh luster to the fame of the international movement. Those Russian comrades of ours have made greater sacrifices, have suffered more, and have shed more heroic blood than any like number of men and women anywhere on earth; they have laid the foundation of the first real democracy that ever drew the breath of life in this world. And the very first act of the triumphant Russian revolution was to proclaim a state of peace with all mankind, coupled with a fervent moral appeal, not to kings, not to emperors, rulers or diplomats but to the people of all nations. Here we have the very breath of democracy, the quintessence of the dawning freedom. The Russian revolution proclaimed its glorious triumph in its ringing and inspiring appeal to the peoples of all the earth. In a humane and fraternal spirit new Russia, emancipated at last from the curse of the centuries, called upon all nations engaged in the frightful war, the Central Powers as well as the Allies, to send representatives to a conference to lay down terms of peace that should be just and lasting. Here was the supreme opportunity to strike the blow to make the world safe for democracy. Was there any response to that noble appeal that in some day to come will be written in letters of gold in the history of the world? Was there any response whatever to that appeal for universal peace? No, not the slightest attention was paid to it by the Christian nations engaged in the terrible slaughter.

It has been charged that Lenin and Trotsky and the leaders of the revolution were treacherous, that they made a traitorous peace with Germany. Let us consider that proposition briefly. At the time of the revolution Russia had been three years in the war. Under the Czar she had lost more than four million of her ill-clad, poorly-equipped, half-starved soldiers, slain outright or disabled on the field of battle. She was absolutely bankrupt. Her soldiers were mainly without arms. This was what was bequeathed to the revolution by the Czar and his regime; and for this condition Lenin and Trotsky were not responsible, nor the Bolsheviki. For this appalling state of affairs the Czar and his rotten bureaucracy were solely responsible. When the Bolsheviki came into power and went through the archives they found and exposed the secret treaties—the treaties that were made between the Czar and the French government, the British government and the Italian government, proposing, after the victory was achieved, to dismember the German Empire and destroy the Central Powers. These treaties have never been denied nor repudiated. Very little has been said about them in the American press. I have a copy of these treaties, showing that the purpose of the Allies is exactly the purpose of the Central Powers, and that is the conquest and spoliation of the weaker nations that has always been the purpose of war.

Wars throughout history have been waged for conquest and plunder. In the Middle Ages when the feudal lords who inhabited the castles whose towers may still be seen along the Rhine concluded to enlarge their domains, to increase their power, their prestige and their wealth they declared war upon one another. But they themselves did not go to war any more than the modern feudal lords, the barons of Wall Street go to war. The feudal barons of the Middle Ages, the economic predecessors of the capitalists of our day, declared all wars. And their miserable serfs fought all the battles. The poor, ignorant serfs had been taught to revere their masters; to believe that when their masters declared war upon one another, it was their patriotic duty to fall upon one another and to cut one another's throats for the profit and glory of the lords and barons who held them in contempt. And that is war in a nutshell. The master class has always declared the wars; the subject class has always fought the battles. The master class has had all to gain and nothing to lose, while the subject class has had nothing to gain and all to lose—especially their lives.

They have always taught and trained you to believe it to be your patriotic duty to go to war and to have yourselves slaughtered at their command. But in all the history of the world you, the people, have never had a voice in declaring war, and strange as it certainly appears, no war by any nation in any age has ever been declared by the people.

And here let me emphasize the fact—and it cannot be repeated too often—that the working class who fight all the battles, the working class who make the supreme sacrifices, the working class who freely shed their blood and furnish the corpses, have never yet had a voice in either declaring war or making peace. It is the ruling class that invariably does both. They alone declare war and they alone make peace.

Yours not to reason why; Yours but to do and die.

That is their motto and we object on the part of the awakening workers of this nation.

If war is right let it be declared by the people. You who have your lives to lose, you certainly above all others have the right to decide the momentous issue of war or peace.

Rose Pastor Stokes! And when I mention her name I take off my hat. Here we have another heroic and inspiring comrade. She had her millions of dollars at command. Did her wealth restrain her an instant? On the contrary her supreme devotion to the cause outweighed all considerations of a financial or social nature. She went out boldly to plead the cause of the working class and they rewarded her high courage with a ten years' sentence to the penitentiary. Think of it! Ten years! What atrocious crime had she committed? What frightful things had she said? Let me answer candidly. She said nothing more than I have said here this afternoon. I want to admit—I want to admit without reservation that if Rose Pastor Stokes is guilty of crime, so am I. If she is guilty for the brave part she has taken in this testing time of human souls I would not be cowardly enough to plead my innocence. And if she ought to be sent to the penitentiary for ten years, so ought I without a doubt.

What did Rose Pastor Stokes say? Why, she said that a government could not at the same time serve both the profiteers and the victims of the profiteers. Is it not true? Certainly it is and no one can successfully dispute it.

Roosevelt said a thousand times more in the very same paper, the *Kansas City Star*. Roosevelt said tauntingly the other day that he would be heard if he went to jail. He knows very well that he is taking no risk of going to jail. He is shrewdly laying his wires for the Republican nomination in 1920 and he is an adept in making the appeal of the demagogue. He would do anything to discredit the Wilson administration that he may give himself and his party all credit. That is the only rivalry there is between the two old capitalist parties — the Republican Party and the Democratic Party — the political twins of the master class. They are not going to have any friction between them this fall. They are all patriots in this campaign, and they are going to combine to prevent the election of any disloyal Socialist. I have never heard anyone tell of any difference between these corrupt capitalist parties. Do you know of any? I certainly do not. The situation is that one is in and the other trying to break in, and that is substantially the only difference between them.

Rose Pastor Stokes never uttered a word she did not have a legal, constitutional right to utter. But her message to the people, the message that stirred their thoughts and opened their eyes — that must be suppressed; her voice must be silenced. And so she was promptly subjected to a mock trial and sentenced to the penitentiary for ten years. Her conviction was a foregone conclusion. The trial of a Socialist in a capitalist court is at best a farcical affair. What ghost of a chance had she in a court with a packed jury and a corporation tool on the bench? Not the least in the world. And so she goes to the penitentiary for ten years if they carry out their brutal and disgraceful graceful program. For my part I do not think they will. In fact I feel sure they will not. If the war were over tomorrow the prison doors would open to our people. They simply mean to silence the voice of protest during the war.

What a compliment it is to the Socialist movement to be thus persecuted for the sake of the truth! The truth alone will make the people free. And for this reason the truth must not be permitted to reach the people. The truth has always been dangerous to the rule of the rogue, the exploiter, the robber. So the truth must be ruthlessly suppressed. That is why they are trying to destroy the Socialist movement; and every time they strike a blow they add a thousand new voices to the hosts proclaiming that socialism is the hope of humanity and has come to emancipate the people from their final form of servitude.

How good this sip of cool water from the hand of a comrade! It is as refreshing as if it were out on the desert waste. And how good it is to look into your glowing faces this afternoon! You are really good looking to me, I assure you. And I am glad there are so many of you. Your tribe has increased amazingly since first I came here. You used to be so few and far between. A few years ago when you struck a town the first thing you had to do was to see if you could locate a Socialist; and you were pretty lucky if you struck the trail of one before you left town. If he happened to be the only one and he is still living, he is now regarded as a pioneer and pathfinder; he holds a place of honor in your esteem, and he has lodgment in the hearts of all who have come after him. It is far different now. You can hardly throw a stone in the dark without hitting a Socialist. They are everywhere in increasing numbers; and what marvelous changes are taking place in the people!

Some years ago I was to speak at Warren in this state. It happened to be at the time that President McKinley was assassinated. In common with all others I deplored that tragic event. There is not a Socialist who would have been guilty of that crime. We do not attack individuals. We do not seek to avenge ourselves upon those opposed to our faith. We have no fight with individuals as such. We are capable of pitying those who hate us. We do not hate them; we know better; we would freely give them a cup of water if they needed it. There is no room in our hearts for hate, except for the system, the social system in which it is possible for one man to amass a stupendous fortune doing nothing, while millions of others suffer and struggle and agonize and die for the bare necessities of existence.

President McKinley, as I have said, had been assassinated. I was first to speak at Portsmouth, having been booked there some time before the assassination. Promptly the Christian ministers of Portsmouth met in special session and passed a resolution declaring that "Debs, more than any other person, was responsible for the assassination of our beloved President." It was due to the doctrine that Debs was preaching that this crime was committed, according to these patriotic parsons, and so this pious gentry, the followers of the meek and lowly Nazarene, concluded that I must not be permitted to enter the city. And they had the mayor issue an order to that effect. I went there soon after, however. I was to speak at Warren, where President McKinley's double-cousin was postmaster. I went there and registered. I was soon afterward invited to leave the hotel. I was exceedingly undesirable that day. I was served with notice that the hall would not be opened and that I would not be permitted to speak. I sent back word to the mayor by the only Socialist left in town — and he only remained because they did not know he was there — I sent word to the mayor that I would speak in Warren that night, according to schedule, or I would leave there in a box for the return turn trip.

The Grand Army of the Republic called a special meeting and then marched to the hall in full uniform and occupied the front seats in order to silence me if my speech did not suit them. I went to the hall, however, found it open, and made my speech. There was no interruption. I told the audience frankly who was responsible for the President's assassination. I said: "As long as there is misery caused by robbery at the bottom there will be assassination at the top." I showed them, evidently to their satisfaction, that it was their own capitalist system that was responsible; the system that had impoverished and brutalized the ancestors of the poor witless boy who had murdered the President. Yes, I made my speech that night and it was well received but when I left there I was still an "undesirable citizen."

Some years later I returned to Warren. It seemed that the whole population was out for the occasion. I was received with open arms. I was no longer a demagogue; no longer a fanatic or an undesirable citizen. I had become exceedingly respectable simply because the Socialists had increased in numbers and socialism had grown in influence and power. If ever I become entirely respectable I shall be quite sure that I have outlived myself.

It is the minorities who have made the history of this world. It is the few who have had the courage to take their places at the front; who have been true enough to themselves to speak the truth that was in them; who have dared oppose the established order of things; who have espoused the cause of the suffering, struggling poor; who have upheld without regard to personal consequences the cause of freedom and righteousness. It is they, the heroic, self-sacrificing few who have made the history of the race and who have paved the way from barbarism to civilization. The many prefer to remain upon the popular side. They lack the courage and vision to join a despised minority that stands for a principle; they have not the moral fiber that withstands, endures and finally conquers. They are to be pitied and not treated with contempt for they cannot help their cowardice. But, thank God, in every age and in every nation there have been the brave and self-reliant few, and they have been sufficient to their historic task; and we, who are here today, are under infinite obligations to them because they suffered, they sacrificed, they went to jail, they had their bones broken upon the wheel, they were burned at the stake and their ashes scattered to the winds by the hands of hate and revenge in their struggle to leave the world better for us than they found it for themselves. We are under eternal obligations to them because of what they did and what they suffered for us and the only way we can discharge that obligation is by doing the best we can for those who are to come after us. And this is the high purpose of every Socialist on earth. Everywhere they are animated by the same lofty principles; everywhere they have the same noble ideals; everywhere they are clasping hands across national boundary lines; everywhere they are calling one another Comrade, the blessed word that springs from the heart of unity and bursts into blossom upon the lips. Each passing day they are getting into closer touch all along the battle line, waging the holy war of the working class of the world against the ruling and exploiting class of the world. They make many mistakes and they profit by them all. They encounter numerous defeats, and grow stronger through them all. They never take a backward step.

The heart of the international Socialist never beats a retreat.

They are pressing forward, here, there and everywhere, in all the zones that girdle the globe. Everywhere these awakening workers, these class-conscious proletarians, these hardy sons and daughters of honest toil are proclaiming the glad tidings of the coming emancipation, everywhere their hearts are attuned to the most sacred cause that ever challenged men and women to action in all the history of the world. Everywhere they are moving toward democracy and the dawn; marching toward the sunrise, their faces all aglow with the light of the coming day. These are the Socialists, the most zealous and enthusiastic crusaders the world has ever known. They are making history that will light up the horizon of coming generations, for their mission is the emancipation of the human race. They have been reviled; they have been ridiculed, persecuted, imprisoned and have suffered death, but they have been sufficient to themselves and their cause, and their final triumph is but a question of time.

Do you wish to hasten the day of victory? Join the Socialist Party! Don't wait for the morrow. Join now! Enroll your name without fear and take your place where you belong. You cannot do your duty by proxy. You have got to do it yourself and do it squarely and then as you look yourself in the face you will have no occasion to blush. You will know what it is to be a real man or woman. You will lose nothing; you will gain everything. Not only will you lose nothing but you will find something of infinite value, and that something will be yourself. And that is your supreme need — to find yourself — to really know yourself and your purpose in life.

You need at this time especially to know that you are fit for something better than slavery and cannon fodder. You need to know that you were not created to work and produce and impoverish yourself to enrich an idle exploiter. You need to know that you have a mind to improve, a soul to develop, and a manhood to sustain.

You need to know that it is your duty to rise above the animal plane of existence. You need to know that it is for you to know something about literature and science and art. You need to know that you are verging on the edge of a great new world. You need to get in touch with your comrades and fellow workers and to become conscious of your interests, your powers and your possibilities as a class. You need to know that you belong to the great majority of mankind. You need to know that as long as you are ignorant, as long as you are indifferent, as long as you are apathetic, unorganized and content, you will remain exactly where you are. You will be exploited; you will be degraded, and you will have to beg for a job. You will get just enough for your slavish toil to keep you in working order, and you will be looked down upon with scorn and contempt by the very parasites that live and luxuriate out of your sweat and unpaid labor.

If you would be respected you have got to begin by respecting yourself. Stand up squarely and look yourself in the face and see a man! Do not allow yourself to fall into the predicament of the poor fellow who, after he had heard a Socialist speech concluded that he too ought to be a Socialist. The argument he had heard was unanswerable. "Yes," he said to himself, "all the speaker said was true and I certainly ought to join the party." But after a while he allowed his ardor to cool and he soberly concluded that by joining the party he might anger his boss and lose his job. He then concluded: "I can't take the chance." That night he slept alone. There was something on his conscience and it resulted in a dreadful dream. Men always have such dreams when they betray themselves. A Socialist is free to go to bed with a clear conscience. He goes to sleep with his manhood and he awakens and walks forth in the morning with his self-respect. He is unafraid and he can look the whole world in the face, without a tremor and without a blush. But this poor weakling who lacked the courage to do the bidding of his reason and conscience was haunted by a startling dream and at midnight he awoke in terror, bounded from his bed and exclaimed: "My God, there is nobody in this room." He was absolutely right. There was nobody in that room.

How would you like to sleep in a room that had nobody in it? It is an awful thing to be nobody. That is certainly a state of mind to get out of, the sooner the better.

There is a great deal of hope for Baker, Ruthenberg and Wagenknecht who are in jail for their convictions; but for the fellow that is nobody there is no pardoning power. He is "in" for life. Anybody can be nobody; but it takes a man to be somebody.

To turn your back on the corrupt Republican Party and the still more corrupt Democratic Party—the gold-dust lackeys of the ruling class counts for still more after you have stepped out of those popular and corrupt capitalist parties to join a minority party that has an ideal, that stands for a principle, and fights for a cause. This will be the most important change you have ever made and the time will come when you will thank me for having made the suggestion. It was the day of days for me. I remember it well. It was like passing from midnight darkness to the noontide light of day. It came almost like a flash and found me ready. It must have been in such a flash that great, seething, throbbing Russia, prepared by centuries of slavery and tears and martyrdom, was transformed from a dark continent to a land of living light.

There is something splendid, something sustaining and inspiring in the prompting of the heart to be true to yourself and to the best you know, especially in a crucial hour of your life. You are in the crucible today, my Socialist comrades! You are going to be tried by fire, to what extent no one knows. If you are weak-fibered and fainthearted you will be lost to the Socialist movement. We will have to bid you goodbye. You are not the stuff of which revolutions are made. We are sorry for you unless you chance to be an "intellectual." The "intellectuals," many of them, are already gone. No loss on our side nor gain on the other.

I am always amused in the discussion of the "intellectual" phase of this question. It is the same old standard under which the rank and file are judged. What would become of the sheep if they had no shepherd to lead them out of the wilderness into the land of milk and honey?

Oh, yes, "I am your shepherd and ye are my mutton."

They would have us believe that if we had no "intellectuals" we would have no movement. They would have our party, the rank and file, controlled by the "intellectual" bosses as the Republican and Democratic parties are controlled. These capitalist parties are managed by "intellectual" leaders and the rank and file are sheep that follow the bellwether to the shambles.

In the Republican and Democratic parties you of the common herd are not expected to think. That is not only unnecessary but might lead you astray. That is what the "intellectual" leaders are for. They do the thinking and you do the voting. They ride in carriages at the front where the band plays and you tramp in the mud, bringing up the rear with great enthusiasm.

The capitalist system affects to have great regard and reward for intellect, and the capitalists give themselves full credit for having superior brains. When we have ventured to say that the time would come when the working class would rule they have bluntly answered "Never! It requires brains to rule." The workers of course have none. And they certainly try hard to prove it by proudly supporting the political parties of their masters under whose administration they are kept in poverty and servitude.

The government is now operating its railroads for the more effective prosecution of the war. Private ownership has broken down utterly and the government has had to come to the rescue. We have always said that the people ought to own the railroads and operate them for the benefit of the people. We advocated that twenty years ago. But the capitalists and their henchmen emphatically objected. "You have got to have brains to run the railroads," they tauntingly retorted. Well, the other day McAdoo, the governor-general of the railroads under government operation; discharged all the high-salaried presidents and other supernumeraries. In other words, he fired the "brains" bodily and yet all the trains have been coming and going on schedule time. Have you noticed any change for the worse since the "brains" are gone? It is a brainless system now, being operated by "hands." But a good deal more efficiently than it had been operated by so-called "brains" before. And this determines infallibly the quality of their vaunted, high-priced capitalist "brains." It is the kind you can get at a reasonable figure at the market place. They have always given themselves credit for having superior brains and given this as the reason for the supremacy of their class. It is true that they have the brains that indicates the cunning of the fox, the wolf, but as for brains denoting real intelligence and the measure of intellectual capacity they are the most woefully ignorant people on earth. Give me a hundred capitalists just as you find them here in Ohio and let me ask them a dozen simple questions about the history of their own country and I will prove to you that they are as ignorant and unlettered as any you may find in the so-called lower class. They know little of history; they are strangers to science; they are ignorant of sociology and blind to art but they know how to exploit, how to gouge, how to rob, and do it with legal sanction. They always proceed legally for the reason that the class which has the power to rob upon a large scale has also the power to control the government and legalize their robbery. I regret that lack of time prevents me from discussing this phase of the question more at length.

They are continually talking about your patriotic duty. It is not their but your patriotic duty that they are concerned about. There is a decided difference. Their patriotic duty never takes them to the firing line or chucks them into the trenches.

And now among other things they are urging you to "cultivate" war gardens, while at the same time a government war report just issued shows that practically 52 percent of the arable, tillable soil is held out of use by the landlords, speculators and profiteers. They themselves do not cultivate the soil. They could not if they would. Nor do they allow others to cultivate it. They keep it idle to enrich themselves, to pocket the millions of dollars of unearned increment. Who is it that makes this land valuable while it is fenced in and kept out of use? It is the people. Who pockets this tremendous accumulation of value? The landlords. And these landlords who toil not and spin not are supreme among American "patriots."

In passing I suggest that we stop a moment to think about the term "landlord." "*Landlord!*" Lord of the Land! The lord of the land is indeed a superpatriot. This lord who practically owns the earth tells you that we are fighting this war to make the world safe for democracy — he who shuts out all humanity from his private domain; he who profiteers at the expense of the people who have been slain and mutilated by multiplied thousands, under pretense of being the great American patriot. It is he, this identical patriot who is in fact the archenemy of the people; it is he that you need to wipe from power. It is he who is a far greater menace to your liberty and your well-being than the Prussian Junkers on the other side of the Atlantic ocean.

Fifty-two percent of the land kept out of use, according to their own figures! They tell you that there is an alarming shortage of flour and that you need to produce more. They tell you further that you have got to save wheat so that more can be exported for the soldiers who are fighting on the other side, while half of your tillable soil is held out of use by the landlords and profiteers. What do you think of that?

Again, they tell you there is a coal famine now in the state of Ohio. The state of Indiana, where I live, is largely underlaid with coal. There is practically an inexhaustible supply. The coal is banked beneath our very feet. It is within touch all about us — all we can possibly use and more. And here are the miners, ready to enter the mines. Here is the machinery ready to be put into operation to increase the output to any desired capacity. And three weeks ago a national officer of the United Mine Workers issued and published a statement to the Labor Department of the United States government to the effect that the 600,000 coal miners in the United States at this time, when they talk about a coal famine, are not permitted to work more than half time. I have been around over Indiana for many years. I have often been in the coal fields; again and again I have seen the miners idle while at the same time there was a scarcity of coal.

They tell you that you ought to buy your coal right away; that you may freeze next winter if you do not. At the same time they charge you three prices for your coal. Oh, yes, this ought to suit you perfectly if you vote the Republican or Democratic ticket and believe in the private ownership of the coal mines and their operation for private profit.

The coal mines now being privately owned, the operators want a scarcity of coal so they can boost their prices and enrich themselves accordingly. If an abundance of coal were mined there would be lower prices and this would not suit the mine owners. Prices soar and profits increase when there is a scarcity of coal.

It is also apparent that there is collusion between the mine owners and the railroads. The mine owners declare there are no cars while the railroad men insist that there is no coal. And between them they delude, defraud and rob the people.

Let us illustrate a vital point. Here is the coal in great deposits all about us; here are the miners and the machinery of production. Why should there be a coal famine upon the one hand and an army of idle and hungry miners on the other hand? Is it not an incredibly stupid situation, an almost idiotic if not criminal state of affairs?

We Socialists say: "Take possession of the mines in the name of the people." Set the miners at work and give every miner the equivalent of all the coal he produces. Reduce the work day in proportion to the development of productive machinery. That would at once settle the matter of a coal famine and of idle miners. But that is too simple a proposition and the people will have none of it. The time will come, however, when the people will be driven to take such action for there is no other efficient and permanent solution of the problem.

In the present system the miner, a wage slave, gets down into a pit 300 or 400 feet deep. He works hard and produces a ton of coal. But he does not own an ounce of it. That coal belongs to some mine-owning plutocrat who may be in New York or sailing the high seas in his private yacht; or he may be hobnobbing with royalty in the capitals of Europe, and that is where most of them were before the war was declared. The industrial captain, so- called, who lives in Paris, London, Vienna or some other center of gaiety does not have to work to revel in luxury. He owns the mines and he might as well own the miners.

That is where you workers are and where you will remain as long as you give your support to the political parties of your masters and exploiters. You vote these miners out of a job and reduce them to corporation vassals and paupers.

We Socialists say: "Take possession of the mines; call the miner to work and return to him the equivalent of the value of his product." He can then build himself a comfortable home; live in it; enjoy it with his family. He can provide himself and his wife and children with clothes—good clothes—not shoddy; wholesome food in abundance, education for the children, and the chance to live the lives of civilized human beings, while at the same time the people will get coal at just what it costs to mine it.

Of course that would be socialism as far as it goes. But you are not in favor of that program. It is too visionary because it is so simple and practical. So you will have to continue to wait until winter is upon you before you get your coal and then pay three prices for it because you insist upon voting a capitalist ticket and giving your support to the present wage-slave system. The trouble with you is that you are still in a capitalist state of mind.

Lincoln said: "If you want that thing, that is the thing you want"; and you will get it to your heart's content. But some good day you will wake up and realize that a change is needed and wonder why you did not know it long before. Yes, a change is certainly needed, not merely a change of party but a change of system; a change from slavery to freedom and from despotism to democracy, wide as the world. When this change comes at last, we shall rise from brutehood to brotherhood, and to accomplish it we have to educate and organize the workers industrially and politically, but not along the zigzag craft lines laid down by Gompers, who through all of his career has favored the master class. You never hear the capitalist press speak of him nowadays except in praise and adulation. He has recently come into great prominence as a patriot. You never find him on the unpopular side of a great issue. He is always conservative, satisfied to leave the labor problem to be settled finally at the banqueting board with Elihu Root, Andrew Carnegie and the rest of the plutocratic civic federationists. When they drink wine and smoke scab cigars together the labor question is settled so far as they are concerned.

And while they are praising Gompers they are denouncing the I.W.W. There are few men who have the courage to say a word in favor of the I.W.W. I have. Let me say here that I have great respect for the I.W.W. Far greater than I have for their infamous detractors.

Listen! There has just been published a pamphlet called "The Truth About the I.W.W." It has been issued after long and thorough investigation by five men of unquestioned standing in the capitalist world. At the head of these investigators was Professor John Graham Brooks of Harvard University, and next to him John A. Fish of the Survey of the Religious Organizations of Pittsburgh, and Mr. Bruere, the government investigator. Five of these prominent men conducted an impartial examination of the I.W.W. To quote their own words they "followed its trail." They examined into its doings beginning at Bisbee where the "patriots," the cowardly business men, the arch-criminals, made up the mob that deported 1,200 workingmen under the most brutal conditions, charging them with being members of the I.W.W. when they knew it to be false.

It is only necessary to label a man "I.W.W." to have him lynched as they did Praeger, an absolutely innocent man. He was a Socialist and bore a German name, and that was his crime. A rumor was started that he was disloyal and he was promptly seized and lynched by the cowardly mob of so-called "patriots."

War makes possible all such crimes and outrages. And war comes in spite of the people. When Wall Street says war the press says war and the pulpit promptly follows with its Amen. In every age the pulpit has been on the side of the rulers and not on the side of the people. That is one reason why the preachers so fiercely denounce the I.W.W.

Take the time to read this pamphlet about the I.W.W. Don't take the word of Wall Street and its press as final. Read this report by five impartial and highly reputable men who made their investigation to know the truth, and that they might tell the truth to the American people. They declare that the I.W.W. in all its career never committed as much violence against the ruling class as the ruling class has committed against the I.W.W.

You are not now reading any reports in the daily press about the trial at Chicago, are you? They used to publish extensive reports when the trial first began, and to prate about what they proposed to prove against the I.W.W. as a gigantic conspiracy against the government. The trial has continued until they have exhausted all their testimony and they have not yet proven violence in a single instance. No, not one! They are utterly without incriminating testimony and yet 112 men are in the dock after lying in jail for months without the shadow of a crime upon them save that of belonging to the I.W.W. That is enough it would seem to convict any man of any crime and send his body to prison and his soul to hell. Just whisper the name of the I.W.W. and you are branded as a disloyalist. And the reason for this is wholly to the credit of the I.W.W., for whatever may be charged against it the I.W.W. has always fought for the bottom dog. And that is why Haywood is despised and prosecuted while Gompers is lauded and glorified by the same gang.

Now what you workers need is to organize, not along craft lines but along revolutionary industrial lines. All of you workers in a given industry, regardless of your trade or occupation, should belong to one and the same union.

Political action and industrial action must supplement and sustain each other. You will never vote the Socialist republic into existence. You will have to lay its foundations in industrial organization. The industrial union is the forerunner of industrial democracy. In the shop where the workers are associated is where industrial democracy has its beginning. Organize according to your industries! Get together in every department of industrial service! United and acting together for the common good your power is invincible.

When you have organized industrially you will soon learn that you can manage as well as operate industry. You will soon realize that you do not need the idle masters and exploiters. They are simply parasites. They do not employ you as you imagine but you employ them to take from you what you produce, and that is how they function in industry. You can certainly dispense with them in that capacity. You do not need them to depend upon for your jobs. You can never be free while you work and live by their sufferance. You must own your own tools and then you will control your own jobs, enjoy the products of your own labor and be free men instead of industrial slaves.

Organize industrially and make your organization complete. Then unite in the Socialist Party. Vote as you strike and strike as you vote.

Your union and your party embrace the working class. The Socialist Party expresses the interests, hopes and aspirations of the toilers of all the world.

Get your fellow workers into the industrial union and the political party to which they rightly belong, especially this year, this historic year in which the forces of labor will assert themselves as they never have before. This is the year that calls for men and women who have courage, the manhood and womanhood to do their duty.

Get into the Socialist Party and take your place in its ranks; help to inspire the weak and strengthen the faltering, and do your share to speed the coming of the brighter and better day for us all.

When we unite and act together on the industrial field and when we vote together on election day we shall develop the supreme power of the one class that can and will bring permanent peace to the world. We shall then have the intelligence, the courage and the power for our great task. In due time industry will be organized on a cooperative basis. We shall conquer the public power. We shall then transfer the title deeds of the railroads, the telegraph lines, the mines, mills and great industries to the people in their collective capacity; we shall take possession of all these social utilities in the name of the people. We shall then have industrial democracy. We shall be a free nation whose government is of and by and for the people.

And now for all of us to do our duty! The clarion call is ringing in our ears and we cannot falter without being convicted of treason to ourselves and to our great cause.

Do not worry over the charge of treason to your masters, but be concerned about the treason that involves yourselves. Be true to yourself and you cannot be a traitor to any good cause on earth.

Yes, in good time we are going to sweep into power in this nation and throughout the world. We are going to destroy all enslaving and degrading capitalist institutions and re-create them as free and humanizing institutions. The world is daily changing before our eyes. The sun of capitalism is setting; the sun of socialism is rising. It is our duty to build the new nation and the free republic. We need industrial and social builders. We Socialists are the builders of the beautiful world that is to be. We are all pledged to do our part. We are inviting—aye challenging you this afternoon in the name of your own manhood and womanhood to join us and do your part.

In due time the hour will strike and this great cause triumphant—the greatest in history—will proclaim the emancipation of the working class and the brotherhood of all mankind.

Statement to the Court Upon Being Convicted of Violating the Sedition Act

September 18, 1918

Your Honor, years ago I recognized my kinship with all living beings, and I made up my mind that I was not one bit better than the meanest on earth. I said then, and I say now, that while there is a lower class, I am in it, and while there is a criminal element I am of it, and while there is a soul in prison, I am not free.

I listened to all that was said in this court in support and justification of this prosecution, but my mind remains unchanged. I look upon the Espionage Law as a despotic enactment in flagrant conflict with democratic principles and with the spirit of free institutions...

Your Honor, I have stated in this court that I am opposed to the social system in which we live; that I believe in a fundamental change—but if possible by peaceable and orderly means...

Standing here this morning, I recall my boyhood. At fourteen I went to work in a railroad shop; at sixteen I was firing a freight engine on a railroad. I remember all the hardships and privations of that earlier day, and from that time until now my heart has been with the working class. I could have been in Congress long ago. I have preferred to go to prison...

I am thinking this morning of the men in the mills and the factories; of the men in the mines and on the railroads. I am thinking of the women who for a paltry wage are compelled to work out their barren lives; of the little children who in this system are robbed of their childhood and in their tender years are seized in the remorseless grasp of Mammon and forced into the industrial dungeons, there to feed the monster machines while they themselves are being starved and stunted, body and soul. I see them dwarfed and diseased and their little lives broken and blasted because in this high noon of Christian civilization money is still so much more important than the flesh and blood of childhood. In very truth gold is god today and rules with pitiless sway in the affairs of men.

In this country—the most favored beneath the bending skies—we have vast areas of the richest and most fertile soil, material resources in inexhaustible abundance, the most marvelous productive machinery on earth, and millions of eager workers ready to apply their labor to that machinery to produce in abundance for every man, woman, and child—and if there are still vast numbers of our people who are the victims of poverty and whose lives are an unceasing struggle all the way from youth to old age, until at last death comes to their rescue and lulls these hapless victims to dreamless sleep, it is not the fault of the Almighty: it cannot be charged to nature, but it is due entirely to the outgrown social system in which we live that ought to be abolished not only in the interest of the toiling masses but in the higher interest of all humanity...

I believe, Your Honor, in common with all Socialists, that this nation ought to own and control its own industries. I believe, as all Socialists do, that all things that are jointly needed and used ought to be jointly owned – that industry, the basis of our social life, instead of being the private property of a few and operated for their enrichment, ought to be the common property of all, democratically administered in the interest of all...

I am opposing a social order in which it is possible for one man who does absolutely nothing that is useful to amass a fortune of hundreds of millions of dollars, while millions of men and women who work all the days of their lives secure barely enough for a wretched existence.

This order of things cannot always endure. I have registered my protest against it. I recognize the feebleness of my effort, but, fortunately, I am not alone. There are multiplied thousands of others who, like myself, have come to realize that before we may truly enjoy the blessings of civilized life, we must reorganize society upon a mutual and cooperative basis; and to this end we have organized a great economic and political movement that spreads over the face of all the earth.

There are today upwards of sixty millions of Socialists, loyal, devoted adherents to this cause, regardless of nationality, race, creed, color, or sex. They are all making common cause. They are spreading with tireless energy the propaganda of the new social order. They are waiting, watching, and working hopefully through all the hours of the day and the night. They are still in a minority. But they have learned how to be patient and to bide their time. They feel – they know, indeed – that the time is coming, in spite of all opposition, all persecution, when this emancipating gospel will spread among all the peoples, and when this minority will become the triumphant majority and, sweeping into power, inaugurate the greatest social and economic change in history.

In that day we shall have the universal commonwealth — the harmonious cooperation of every nation with every other nation on earth...

Your Honor, I ask no mercy and I plead for no immunity. I realize that finally the right must prevail. I never so clearly comprehended as now the great struggle between the powers of greed and exploitation on the one hand and upon the other the rising hosts of industrial freedom and social justice.

I can see the dawn of the better day for humanity. The people are awakening. In due time they will and must come to their own.

When the mariner, sailing over tropic seas, looks for relief from his weary watch, he turns his eyes toward the southern cross, burning luridly above the tempest-vexed ocean. As the midnight approaches, the southern cross begins to bend, the whirling worlds change their places, and with starry finger-points the Almighty marks the passage of time upon the dial of the universe, and though no bell may beat the glad tidings, the lookout knows that the midnight is passing and that relief and rest are close at hand. Let the people everywhere take heart of hope, for the cross is bending, the midnight is passing, and joy cometh with the morning.

The American Labor Party

February 21, 1925

The progressive tendencies in American politics are the outgrowth of the final stages of American capitalism and reflect the political awakening of the American working class.

These tendencies, despite all the attempts through the blind stupidity of the workers and the covert machinations of their enemies to thwart or misdirect them, will inevitably lead to and result in the formation of an American labor party.

When?

We do not know. I hope soon. But sooner or later it will come. That I know if I have teamed anything at all about the operation of the resistless forces that are centralizing capital, socializing industry, organizing and arraying the workers against their exploiting masters, and compelling them more and more to take the initiative in the intensifying struggle growing out of their antagonistic economic interests, which can end only with their complete industrial emancipation.

This struggle is political as well as economic and will, because it must, be fought out accordingly, and this can only be done when labor has a political party as well as an economic union of its own to express its interests, declare its aims, and develop its power to fight its battles and achieve its victory.

This does not mean that a labor party shall consist exclusively of workers but it does mean that all who enter its ranks do so with the understanding that it is a labor party, not a middle class party, not a reform party, nor a progressive party (of which the Republican and Democratic parties are shining examples) but an open-and-above-board labor party, standing squarely on a labor platform, and marshalling its forces to fight labor's political battles for industrial freedom.

Most earnestly do I hope such a party will result from the Conference for Progressive Political Action to be held at Chicago beginning February 21st in pursuance of the agreement of the Conference to follow up the progressive campaign with a permanent party organization.

To be frank I shall have to confess, not without reluctance, that I have not the faith I should like to have in a consummation so devoutly to be wished. But whatever the outcome I shall not be disappointed. I have long since gotten over that and learned how to wait.

We can have no effective labor party without the backing and support of the labor unions. That is a fact without question. The present leaders of the unions, strange as it certainly appears, are almost to a man opposed to a labor party. In this they are in entire accord with the capitalist masters and labor exploiters.

The hope for an American labor party lies not in the official labor leaders but in the rank and file, and until the latter are aroused, insist upon, and compel independent political action, no such a craft can be successfully launched upon the foul and stagnant waters of American politics.

If a bona fide labor party cannot be organized at Chicago then I hope that no party at all will issue from that conference. Better far no party than a nondescript imitation of one, composed of so-called progressive and reform elements, more or less muddled, discordant, and wholly lacking in clear aim, definite object, and concerted purpose.

A "third party" of such a nature would at best align the dwindling "little interests" against the "big interests," seek to patch up and prolong the present corrupt and collapsing capitalist system, and failing utterly to effect any material change or achieve any substantial benefit would finally fizzle out and add one more to the list of "third party" fiascoes.

A political party to succeed, for good or evil, must express, in the main, identical economic interests, without which there is no foundation to build or stand upon. A third party at this advanced stage of our industrial and social development, unless it stood expressly for labor, would be lacking such a foundation and consequently could not endure. Only a labor party can now be organized as a third party with any hope whatever of permanence and achieving its object.

A political party today must stand for labor and the freedom of labor, or it must stand for capital and the exploitation of labor. It cannot possibly stand for both any more than it could for both freedom and slavery.

I want to see the workers of this nation rise in the might of their intelligence and demand a party of their own, free, eternally free from the paralyzing putridities of the parties of their silk-hatted, wealth-inflated, job-owning and labor-exploiting masters — a party with a backbone and the courage to stand up without apology and proclaim itself a Labor Party, clean, confident of its own inherent powers, bearing proudly the union label in token of its fundamental conquering principle of industrial and political solidarity, and challenging the whole world of capitalism to contest the right of this nation to own its own industries, to control its own economic and social life, and the right of the toiling and producing masses to own their own jobs, to enjoy the fruits of their own labor, and to be the masters of their own lives.

I am suspicious of those who admit that we must have a labor party but object to having it called by its right name. It should be a matter of pride and certainly not of shame to a labor party to have its true title nailed to its masthead.

If not, why not? Shall we fear to keep out many who would otherwise join? That is the very reason the party should be known for what it actually is as well as what it actually stands for. We must bear no false label, carry no false banner, nor seek support under any false pretense whatsoever.

We must stand avowedly, face front, for labor—for the people who produce, who render needed service, and who are useful and necessary to the world.

We need not designate both industrial labor and farm labor in naming our party. Both are labor, alike useful, productive, and necessary, subject to the same oppression and the same exploitation, and bound to be united in one political solidarity in the same political party.

It is a fact amazing as it is humiliating that the workers of the United States, the most advanced industrial nation on the globe, are practically the only ones who have no political party of their own, being content to give their support to the corrupt and enslaving parties of their masters, and meekly bowing their necks to the yoke of injunction rule. Every other nation large and small with scarcely an exception has its labor party in full panoply fighting its political battles for emancipation. Even Mexico, so long reviled by our one hundred percent morons as the land of "greasers" and peonage, has its militant labor movement to shame us into getting into line with the advancing columns of International Labor's Grand Army of Emancipation.

Let me make it clear that I am not wanting another socialist party organized. We already have one and that is enough. Neither do I want another capitalist party organized, having already two, more than enough.

A middle-class party, by whatever name, would still be a capitalist party, for while it might champion "little interests" against "big interests," with a sop to labor, it would still stand for the capitalist system and the perpetuation of wage-slavery.

If a genuine labor party is organized at Chicago I shall not expect the platform to go the limit of radical demands but shall be satisfied with a reasonable statement of labor's rights and interests as well as its duties and responsibilities, doubting not that with the progress of the party its platform will in due time embrace every essential feature of the working class program for deliverance from industrial servitude.

The Socialist party can, should, and I have no doubt will join such a party wholeheartedly, becoming an integral part of its structure, reserving, however, its autonomy unimpaired and using all its powers and functions in building up, equipping, promoting, and directing the general party.

To this end the Socialist party must stand fearless and erect, inflexible and uncompromising for the working class upon the basis of the class struggle and wage the war against capitalism for the liberation of labor from its age-old bondage.

In the event of failure to organize a labor party with which we can consistently affiliate, I shall hope and strive for the continuance of the Conference for Progressive Political Action and its sessions and deliberations from time to time until it shall finally culminate, as it eventually must, in the AMERICAN LABOR PARTY.

Speech at 1925 Conference for Progressive Political Action

February 21, 1925, Lexington Hotel, Chicago, IL

Fellow Delegates and Friends:

I appreciate fully the very cordial reception you tendered with such marked enthusiasm, but I don't forget that this high compliment is paid to the cause that I have been endeavoring to serve and to me personally not at all.

I wish that you were all Socialists. But I realize that a great many of you are not. I hope I have never been and never shall be narrow enough and bigoted enough to deny any human being the same right to his or her honest conviction and the same right to express these convictions and stand up and fight for them that I shall claim for myself.

There are, as I see it, two paramount questions before this body. The first is, shall a new party be organized, and secondly, if a new party is organized, what kind of party shall it be?

It is quite natural that there should be a very wide divergence of opinion as to these questions. It would be a miracle almost if the delegates composing this great body, representing so many different elements and constituents, were of one mind, of one purpose, as to the questions that confront them for consideration and action.

Speaking for myself and my colleagues, I favor the organization, here and now, of a new party. I also stand, in addition to the demand for a new party, that this shall be a party of the working class.

A party in this later day of our industrial and social development is either a capitalist party or it is a labor party. It is the one or the other. It cannot be both. We all know that in the evolution of industry and of society there has been a division of society, and that today it consists mainly of two economic classes,

The capitalist class upon the one hand and upon the other the working class; and these two classes, whether you admit it or not, are pitted against each other, not only in this country, but throughout the world, in an irrepressible struggle. These two classes can never be permanently harmonized or reconciled. It is this that is called the class struggle, that is shaking the foundations of the whole civilized world.

This is an age of organization. Working men realize this in having organized pretty thoroughly upon the industrial field in pitting themselves against the organized power of their masters and their exploiters. They have yet to learn that the labor question is essentially a political question. If they find it necessary to unite upon the industrial field, to unite and strike together, how can they consistently fight each other at the ballot box?

Politics is simply the expression in political terms of the economic interests of certain groups or classes. The masters and exploiters realize this fact and they are in politics, not in non-partisan politics, but in politics.

I have heard some allusions to non-partisan political organization. That is to say, a political party that is not a political party. I know of no organization, no political organization, that is or can be non-partisan. It is a question, as we believe, mainly of the education of the working class, and here let me say that my interpretation of the working class includes all useful workers of brain and brawn, all who usefully serve society in any trade, occupation, or profession. All of these properly belong to the working class. I draw the line at the exploiters and the parasites and there I draw it sharply.

Now it has been said that the time has not yet come to organize a new party, and when, I venture to ask, will that time come?

It was my good fortune to personally know the founder and Grand Chief, the first Grand Chief of the Brotherhood of Locomotive Engineers, to personally know the first Grand Master of the Brotherhood of Locomotive Fireman. How often I have heard both of them tell of their early experiences in the efforts they made to lay the foundation of the organization of their class. There were but a handful of men who organized these two great brotherhoods. They were told that the time had not come for such work and everything possible was done to discourage them, but they were of such fiber, such moral fiber, that they had the courage to stand erect, to assert themselves, and to make the beginning that resulted in these great organizations.

Every great human movement has a small beginning in every age, in every nation. There have been a few heroic souls, women and men, who have ideas in advance of their time, who have had the courage to give expression to these ideas, to stand staunchly in their advocacy and to pave their way by their heroism, by their self-sacrifice to better conditions for mankind.

It was my pleasure, as well as my honor, to be with that magnificent woman, Susan B. Anthony, almost a half century ago, when she came to the town in which I lived, in response to an invitation that I had extended to her to advocate the cause of women's rights. I remember in escorting her from the station to the hotel how she was sneered at by passersby, who felt insulted that this brazen creature had been permitted to enter that community. I recall it all so vividly as I stand here in your presence this afternoon; all of the influences surrounding her were brought to bear to prevent her from advocating the right of women to take part in the affairs of society. They declared that the time had not come for it. They declared that it was impossible. They made all sorts of arguments to discourage Susan B. Anthony, and Elizabeth Cady Stanton, these magnificent women whose names are in history, the glory of their sex. It was a small beginning they made, but they had the courage to make it, and they have written their names in indelible letters in the annals of mankind. We may not be able to make a very great beginning here, but the important thing is that we shall make a beginning.

I have said that a party is either a capitalist party or it is a labor party. I deny that any party can by any possible means serve both these classes with the same fidelity. It is absolutely impossible. If a party serves the capitalist exploiter it is at the expense of his exploited victim, and if a party serves the exploited worker it is at the expense of his economic master.

Much has been said about wresting the power of monopoly from the hands of the few who hold sway in our affairs. Let it be understood that the economic power is always and everywhere the political ruler. How are you going to wrest this power from the hands of the autocracy, who are in the minority, unless you organize the workers and their sympathizers, who are in the majority, unless you educate and organize the masses? And build up the political power that will wrest from them the power they have to oppress and exploit the people by taking from them the private ownership of the instruments of production that make them the economic masters and the political rulers of the nation?

The question for us to consider is simply this: are or are we not in favor of this nation owning and controlling its own industries? That is the fundamental question. That is what confronts this body. As long as you permit a relative few to privately own the sources and means of wealth, the tools of production, they will be in power. You will be in servitude. You will produce the wealth and they will have it under whatever administration you may have. They will do nothing and you will have that, and that is what you have been getting under the administration of both the Republican and Democratic parties all of these years.

Now if what has been charged against these two parties by this body, by this conference, if the half of what has been charged, is true, then these parties are hopelessly corrupt and reactionary, and how can the great body of people who are oppressed and exploited and degraded, how can they hope for any relief by timidly approaching the doors of these corrupt parties and begging for some slight consideration, and be treated with contempt?

The class now in power cannot rule honestly. They must rule corruptly. They are in the minority. They have not the votes of their own to put them in power, but they have the money with which to corrupt the electorate. They have the money with which to corrupt the courts and to buy the legislators, and to debauch all our institutions. They have the power to do this because they have the money, and they have the money because they own the means of production and distribution. The great mass of the workers depend upon them for employment. In this system no working man - we boast of every man having the right to life, liberty, and the pursuit of happiness, and yet in this system that has been alternately supported by both of the capitalist parties, no man has a right to work. He can only work on conditions that the master who owns the tools he works with grants him permission to work, and the man who works by permission lives by permission, and is in no sense a free man.

Now we make the claim that the time has come for the great body of the workers and those who sympathize with them to organize a new party and to begin the work of extending the operation and activities of this party all over the country. We can make the beginning here.

We can start forth with a message. We can make the appeal that will ring all over this country, and I am satisfied that hundreds of thousands of the workers will respond to that appeal. But the great mass of the people are not articulate. They have no means of making themselves heard. If the question of organizing a new party, and that party being a labor party, if that question were submitted to the great body of the American workers, I am satisfied that a very large proportion of them would vote in favor of launching a new party.

There are those present—I concede their honesty—I impugn no man's motive—there are those present who believe that a kind of middle party can be organized that will embrace so many more of the people. They indulge the illusion that it is possible to permanently unite men whose interests are in conflict. It cannot be done. It is an impossible undertaking. I venture to say that if this body in the course of its deliberations decides upon organizing a middle class party that shall be neither one thing or the other, but that shall have progress for its shibboleth, that shall be known as a progressive party—and by the way—do you know of a party that is not a progressive party? I don't.

Do you know of any man or woman in this country who will confess himself or herself a reactionary? I don't. Rockefeller is a progressive. So is Morgan. So are all the rest of them progressive, and there is not a term in our vocabulary that has been more prostituted in the last few years than the term progressive. Now, what does it mean? Absolutely nothing.

Make your appeal broad enough to embrace small capitalists and workers and all sorts of elements, launch that party tomorrow, and I admit that it may make some little progress. I admit that it may have some small accession to its ranks, but it cannot live. Its death is a foregone conclusion. Organize a so-called progressive party combining all of these elements, more or less in conflict with each other, and they soon begin to disintegrate and they will go the way that all third parties have gone during the last fifty years.

A labor party is the only party that can be organized with any hope of making it a permanent party and achieving its historic mission.

It is a fortunate fact that the workers everywhere are beginning to open their eyes at last, beginning to realize that they have brains as well as hands, that they can think as well as work, that they are fit for something better than slavery and for cannon fodder. They are beginning to stand erect here and there and everywhere all along the line, beginning to realize that what is done for them must be done by themselves. And so they are gradually developing their self-reliance and they are making the appeal to their own solidarity.

They are still in the minority, and here let it be observed that every great movement in its inception was not only in the minority, unpopular, consisting of those who had ideas and courage, who did their work and rendered their service to humanity, these awakened and awakening and intelligent and awakening workers are still in the minority, but they are in alliance with the force of evolution, and as certain as I stand in your presence this afternoon, this minority will be converted in course of time into the triumphant majority and sweep into power and seize the reins of government in the name of the people and transfer the title deeds from the Rockefellers, Goulds, Vanderbilts, and Morgans to the people in their collective capacity, and then for the first time we will have democracy and self-government in the history of this Republic.

Ah, but this is far-fetched, some of you seem to think, and possibly it is. But it is the only issue before this body that is worthy of serious consideration. This is a movement that is making progress.

Now the workers have organized to a very large extent industrially. They are beginning to realize their interests, their power, their duty, their responsibility as a class now. I know that it is not very popular in the presence of some people to talk about classes. We are supposed to be a classless country. There are no classes in the United States. We are all in the same class with Rockefeller and the rest of them, and we prove it by voting that ticket on election day.

Now, Rockefeller and Morgan and Gary and the rest of them, believe me, are class conscious. I only wish the workers were as class conscious as are these great exploiting Capitalists.

The power that they have over people never can be abolished while they are in possession of the instruments that give them that power. That is the private ownership of the means of our common life. They own the railroads; they own the telegraph, the telephone; they own all these great agencies of production and distribution, the mines and the mills and the factories that have been socially produced, that are socially operated, that are socially necessary and still are held in private hands. The owners of the railroads have nothing to do with their operation. If every owner of an American railroad took a ship, an airship tonight, and left this planet, the people would never know it, for every train would come and go on time, and so with all of the great industries. Their private owners have no more to do with their management or their operation than if they lived upon Mars. Now, if the people, in their collective capacity can develop these great industries, if they can operate them socially, and if their very lives depend upon them, can't they also develop intelligence enough to make themselves the owners and the masters of these industries and operate them, not to produce multimillionaires and billionaires, but to produce wealth in abundance for all of the people?

Poverty amid plenty. Is it not strange that in this land of fabulous abundance there is such widespread poverty and misery that defies the power of all language to properly describe? Here in America we live in perhaps the most favored land beneath the bending skies, vast areas of the richest and most fertile soil, all of the raw materials in inexhaustible abundance, the most marvelous productive machinery on the face of the globe, and the million of workers, men and women and children, aye children, two million of them still having their puny bodies coined into the capitalist profit, is infinitely more important than the working man's life.

Is it not strange that in this land of fabulous plenty there is still so much poverty, so many million of our people whose life consists of a long, hard, fierce struggle all the way from youth to age and at last death comes to the rescue and stills the aching heart and lulls that victim to dreamless sleep.

This all seems very strange to me, in one aspect of it, but not in another, for I have learned enough to know in my experience and observation that that very limited class that owns and controls the means of our common life not only controls the government in every department and has the injunctions issued under both Republican and Democratic administrations that paralyzes labor unions; they not only control the government in every department, but they control all of our educational institutions, they have the power to penalize, to proscribe, to exile the workers by discharging and black-listing the men, the best among them, for the reason they have intelligence enough and courage enough to stand up for the interests of their classes. They have the power to control the education, a large part of which consists of mis-education, the purpose of which is to keep the people in ignorance and, through their ignorance, in servitude.

Shakespeare was right when he said, "There is no darkness but ignorance and there is no slavery but ignorance," and that is the trouble with the American people, and the average politician tells them that he is so proud to stand in their presence, to look in their intelligent faces, he flatters their ignorance to keep them ignorant, while upon the other hand, the Socialist agitator has made himself an undesirable citizen, despised and persecuted, because he has the courage to tell the workers that they are ignorant and that they will remain where they are so long as they are ignorant, indifferent, and unorganized. He tells them about the class struggle, not because he is in favor of classes, quite the contrary, because he is opposed to classes and wants to put an end to the class struggle.

The capitalist, upon the other hand, tries to obscure it in every way possible. He'd not have the workers realize it and that is why the great majority of them remain in the parties of their masters. Who is it that votes the Republican party and the Democratic party into power? It is the working class. The capitalist doesn't vote a working class ticket, but the working class do vote the capitalist ticket, and that is why the capitalists are in power and the workers in servitude, and we want to reverse this situation and put the workers in power, and that is what will come to pass with a triumph of this great movement that I hope to see inaugurated here in the form of a new political party that stands foursquare to all the storms that blow for the working class, and those who sympathize with them in their heroic struggle for industrial emancipation, and it is coming.

As I stand here this afternoon, looking into your faces, many of whom are so familiar to me, I congratulate myself for being here. I feel all the better for being in a little nearer touch with those with whom I have disagreed and who have disagreed with me. I feel that it is so far better for us to be at least on decent human terms with each other, no matter how widely we may disagree, far better this than to be pitted against each other in hostile camps, wasting our time in abusing each other.

Now I have every respect for every one of this movement who is looking forward or who thinks he is looking forward. He is proceeding according to his light. I would do nothing under any circumstances to discourage the tendency, the progressive tendency of this movement. I would not utter a word to reflect upon any man or woman, any delegate in this body who, however reactionary they may seem to me, believe that they are looking forward and in their heart desire to be progressive.

I would encourage all of these tendencies and that is why the Socialist Party became affiliated with this Conference, not for the purpose of being absorbed or absorbing the Conference, but for the purpose of helping along, for the purpose of helping in the work of education and organization, encouraging those who don't yet see their way clear to come to the Socialist movement, and this Conference, whatever may be the outcome, my friends, is going to leave something that will have a permanent place in the annals of our nation. It is going to result in some good. We may leave here more or less disappointed. No matter. The very fact that this Conference has been possible is sufficient evidence to my mind that it is going to result in some good. It is the beginning. It will have its continuance. It is a more or less logical development. It will lead to something else, and in the right direction, and so I am very glad I am here, and have had the privilege of meeting those who are here, many of them with whom I have hitherto been in disagreement.

Now I believe that it is impossible to compromise a principle, and the Socialist Party is committed to a certain principle. To compromise principle is to court death and disaster. It is better to be true to a principle and to stand alone and be able to look yourself in the face without a blush, far better to be in a hopeless minority than to be in a great popular and powerful majority of the unthinking.

Do you know that all the progress in this whole world's history has been made by minorities? I have somehow been fortunately all of my life in the minority. I have thought again and again that if I ever find myself in the majority I will know that I have outlived myself. There is something magnificent about having the courage to stand with a few with and for a principle and to fight for it without fear or favor, developing all of your latent power, expanding to the proportional end, rising to your true stature, no matter whose respect you may forfeit, as long as you keep your own.

I am glad to stand with a staunch revolutionary minority, and the capitalists understand what we are and what we stand for, even if the workers don't. They don't object in the least to the organization of a third party. They know very well it will not last very long, but they are decidedly opposed to the organization of a labor party. That is what they are opposed to, and if a labor party is organized, it must expect from the very beginning to be misrepresented and ridiculed and traduced in every possible way, but if it consists of those who are the living representatives of its principles it will make progress in spite of them, and in due course of time it will sweep into triumph.

So I have learned to be patient and to bide the time. I am expecting something from this body before it adjourns. But let me say to you, whether I receive what I expect or not, I shall not leave here disappointed. Long, long ago in my life I learned how to refuse to be disappointed. No one can disappoint me but myself, and I refuse to betray myself. I can't do that. I prefer to be on speaking terms with myself, and so I stand for this principle. Make the appeal to the working class on this principle.

You workers of brain and brawn, it is you and you alone who support the government and conserve all civilization. Were it not for you, the whole social fabric would collapse in an instant. It is you who do the work, the useful work. It is you who produce the wealth, every ounce, every dollar of it, you who support the government and conserve civilization. You have but to realize this to awaken to the necessity of unifying your forces all along the line, taking counsel of yourselves, cultivating self-reliance, closing up the industrial ranks, the political ranks, striking together, standing together in every hour of conflict, every hour of strife, and in due course of time the hour will strike, your day will have come, you will sweep into power and you will issue for the first time in human history the proclamation of the emancipation of the workers and the true civilization of all mankind.

CPSIA information can be obtained
at www.ICGtesting.com
Printed in the USA
BVOW08s0521140517
484036BV00009B/159/P